WHITE STAR
LINE

Also by Deborah Hopkinson

UP BEFORE DAYBREAK
Cotton and People in America

SHUTTING OUT THE SKY
Life in the Tenements of New York, 1880–1924

TITANIC

VOICES FROM THE DISASTER

BY
DEBORAH
HOPKINSON

SCHOLASTIC
FOCUS

NEW YORK

No.	Words.	Origin. Station:	
To		Titanic	

CQD SOS SOS CQD

We are sinking
being put into

M. / 18___

d — m G Y

ast passengers in

oats

m G Y

L. L. Cennor.

J G Ward.

Copyright © 2012 by Deborah Hopkinson. All rights reserved.
Published by Scholastic Focus, a division of Scholastic Inc.,
Publishers since 1920. SCHOLASTIC, SCHOLASTIC FOCUS, and
associated logos are trademarks and/or registered trademarks of Scholastic Inc.

This book was originally published in hardcover by Scholastic
Press in 2012.

ISBN 978-0-545-11675-6

22 21 20 19 18 17   19 20 21 22 23 24

The text type was set in ITC Avant Garde Gothic.
The display type was set in Bureau Eagle.
Book design by Phil Falco

Printed in the U.S.A. 40
This edition first printing, January 2014

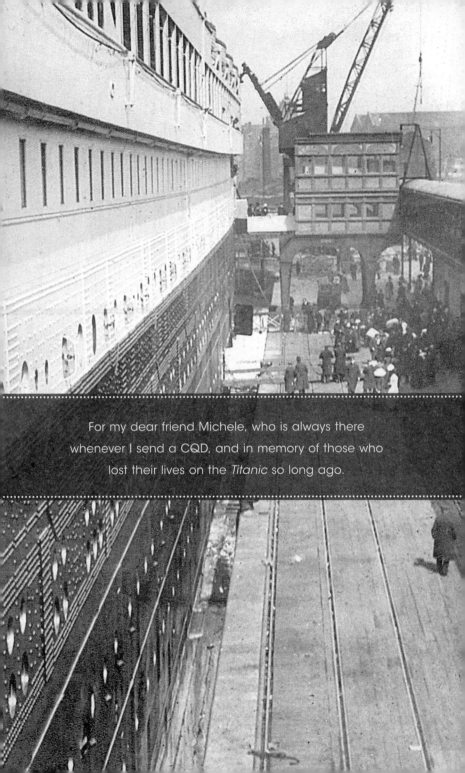

For my dear friend Michele, who is always there whenever I send a CQD, and in memory of those who lost their lives on the *Titanic* so long ago.

⇒ TABLE OF CONTENTS ⇐

The wreck of the *Titanic*.

❄ FOREWORD ❄

At 2:20 a.m. on Monday, April 15, 1912, the RMS *Titanic*, on her glorious maiden voyage from Southampton to New York, sank after striking an iceberg in the North Atlantic, killing 1,496 men, women, and children. A total of 712 survivors escaped with their lives on twenty lifeboats that had room for 1,178 people. There were 2,208 on board.

The loss of life was heartbreaking. It seems unbelievable even today. How did this magnificent ship, the largest and most luxurious in the world, simply disappear in a matter of hours?

Now, in the twenty-first century, the *Titanic* — the ship itself, as well as her passengers and crew, the wreck, and every last detail of the sinking — continues to fascinate us. Perhaps no other disaster in history has been so closely examined, studied by scientists, mariners, and those who research social behavior. It is the subject of websites, articles, discussion boards, films, scientific expeditions, and yes, books like this.

Maybe the *Titanic* makes us all historians. We can't help being curious: What happened? Why? Who said what and when? What did it mean? And, of course, what if?

This book is an introduction to the disaster and to just a few of the people who survived — a stewardess, a nine-year-old boy, a science teacher, a wealthy gentleman, a brave seaman, an American high school senior, a young mother on her way to start a new life, and more.

I hope their stories and voices remind you, as they do me, that our lives are fragile and precious. And I hope they make you wonder, as I do, what it would have been like to be on the *Titanic* that night so long ago. . . .

⇒ DIAGRAM OF THE SHIP ⇐

1. Anchor Crane
2. Crew Quarters
3. Crow's Nest
4. Third Class Berths
5. Bridge
6. Post Office
7. Wheelhouse
8. First Class Staterooms
9. Marconi Room
10. Swimming Baths
11. Forward First Class Grand Staircase
12. First Class Reception
13. Gymnasium
14. Coal Bunkers
15. First Class Staterooms
16. Compass Platform

17. Third Class Dining Room

18. Boiler Room

19. Third Class Kitchen

20. Aft First Class Staircase

21. Reciprocating Engines

22. Kitchen Galley

23. Turbine Engine

24. Library

25. À la Carte Restaurant

26. Café Parisien

27. Fresh Water Tanks

28. Second Class Dining Room

29. Second Class Staterooms

30. Stern Bridge for Docking

31. Third Class Rooms

> *"Mummy! At last we are on the 'lantic."*
> — Frankie Goldsmith, age 9

Crew members carry luggage onto the RMS *Titanic* as passengers board at Queenstown, Ireland, on April 11, 1912.

SETTING SAIL

When an Irish lad named Frank Browne was seventeen, his uncle Robert gave him a camera. Frank fell in love with photography and before long he was snapping that shutter everywhere he went.

Fifteen years later, Frank was a teacher, preparing to become a priest just like his uncle. One day he received a wonderful surprise in the mail — another gift from Uncle Robert. This time it was a once-in-a-lifetime treat — a ticket for a two-day cruise on the maiden voyage of the RMS *Titanic*. First class!

Frank traveled from his home in Dublin, Ireland, to London's Waterloo Station to board the "*Titanic* Special." He rode the first class passenger train, which left at 9:45 a.m. on Wednesday, April 10, 1912, heading for the port of Southampton, about 78 miles away. (An earlier train, for second and third class passengers, had departed bright and early, at 7:30 a.m.) Frank reached the White Star Dock at 11:30 a.m., just in time for the ship's noon departure.

Like so many people that day, Frank could barely contain his excitement. Before him was a breathtaking sight — the largest and most luxurious ship the world had ever seen, a masterpiece of human engineering, class, and comfort.

Not only that, she was safe. The *Titanic*, as everyone knew, was practically unsinkable.

❖

The *Titanic* was built in Belfast, Ireland, by the shipbuilding firm of Harland and Wolff especially for the White Star Line steamship company. Although the airplane had been invented in 1903, it wasn't until the 1950s that regular transatlantic jet service became available. So in 1912, when the *Titanic* sailed, people were still relying on ships to cross the seas, just as they had for centuries.

As the twentieth century dawned, travelers wanted luxurious accommodations on board ships — and reliability. The White Star Line aimed to give its customers the best, and beat out its rival company, the Cunard Line, which had built its own new luxury liner, the *Lusitania*. The *Lusitania* was faster, while White Star's new Olympic class of ships would be designed for comfort first.

3

White Star had been in the passenger ocean liner business since 1867, when Thomas Henry Ismay bought the firm. His son, J. Bruce Ismay, became managing director in 1904 at the age of forty-one. By 1912, White Star was part of a large American holding company controlled by the American financier J. P. Morgan.

When the *Titanic* sailed, J. Bruce Ismay was on board. Along with being managing director of the White Star Line, he served as president of the parent company, International Mercantile Maritime Company (IMM). Ismay essentially worked for J. P. Morgan, one of the richest men in the world. Morgan had planned to go on the maiden voyage but canceled at the last minute. In the end, Ismay may have wished he never went either.

J. Bruce Ismay, chairman and director of the White Star Line, (right) inspects the hull of the *Titanic* with William James Pirrie, the chairman of the shipbuilding firm Harland and Wolff.

CHAPTER ONE

On July 31, 1909, White Star signed an agreement with Harland and Wolff to construct three sister ships: the *Olympic*, the *Titanic*, and a third to follow later. Originally to be called the *Gigantic*, this third ship was eventually named the *Britannic*. The *Britannic* sank in 1916, in even less time than the *Titanic*, after hitting a mine during World War I.

White Star took enormous pride in its new Olympic class of ships. Not only were the ships spacious, they were designed to take advantage of all the modern technology of the early twentieth century, combining luxury with stability. To meet the needs of travelers who wanted speed and reliability as well as comfort, the powerful engines ensured that people arrived at their destinations on time.

The *Olympic* was launched first, making her maiden voyage on June 14, 1911. Construction on the *Titanic* began March 31, 1909. Quality was important — the *Titanic* cost $7.5 million to build. This new ship would look very much like the *Olympic* but would be slightly larger and have several new features, including specially decorated first class staterooms and even a "sidewalk café," the Café Parisien, with real French waiters. When the *Titanic* was registered on March 25, 1912, her weight was listed at 46,328.57 tons — just over a thousand more than the *Olympic*.

She was officially the largest ship in the world.

❧

The *Titanic* was scheduled to leave Belfast for her brief sea trials on Monday, April 1, 1912. High winds postponed the departure until the next morning. That meant one less day in

Southampton to get everything ready — and there was a lot
to do.

Titanic in dry dock in Belfast as she is being built.

Much of the boat had been fitted out in Belfast. During
the years the *Titanic* was built, Harland and Wolff employed
as many as 15,000 workers. The men started work at 7:50 a.m.
and finished at 5:30 p.m., with one ten-minute break and a half
hour for lunch. Just to install the ship's machinery and complete the interior had taken ten months and millions of hours
of work. When the 15½-ton anchor arrived, it was pulled by a
team of twenty horses.

By the time the *Titanic* had left Belfast, the machinery and
furniture were in place, and 3,560 life belts were on board.
But the ship still needed to be loaded with coal, food, cargo,

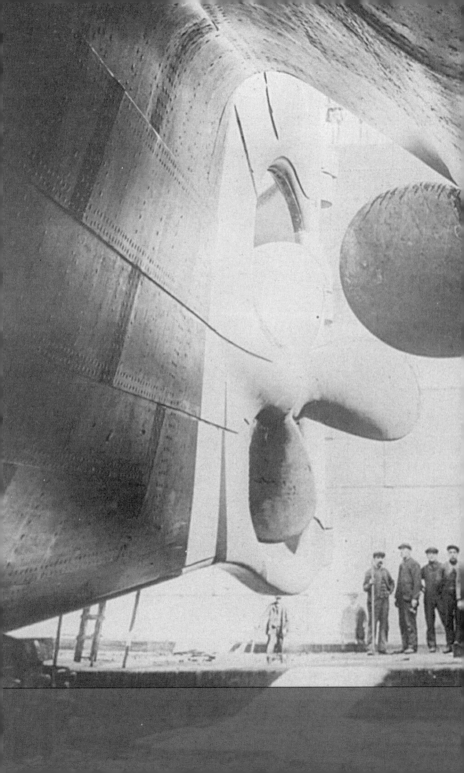

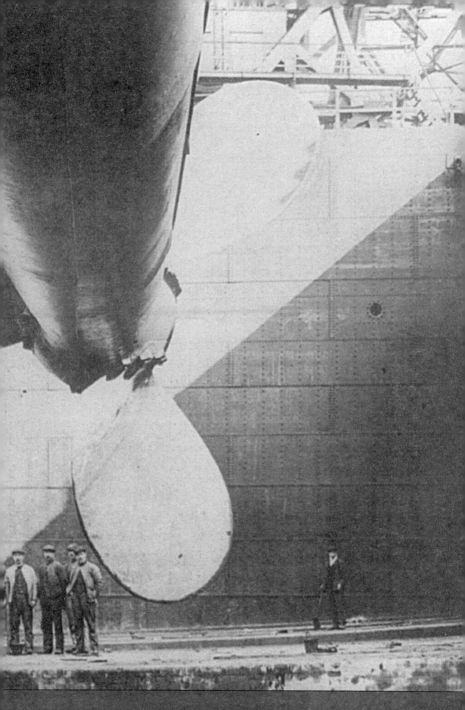

As preparations were made to launch the *Titanic* in May 1911, the ship's giant propellers could be seen.

tableware — and, of course, passengers and their baggage — before setting out for New York on a week-long voyage with more than 2,200 people on board.

The RMS *Titanic* also carried mail. *RMS* stood for "Royal Mail Ship," which meant a ship under contract to carry mail for speedy delivery. The *Titanic* sailed with five Sea Post Office clerks, and more than three thousand mailbags bulging with mail — over seven million pieces. The post office was located on G Deck, with mail storage on the starboard side near the bottom of the ship, on the Orlop Deck.

The ship performed well in her sea trials, which pleased her captain, Edward J. Smith. Captain Smith had been with the company since 1880 and was easily White Star's most popular captain. He was known as the "millionaires' captain" because so many upper-class passengers would only travel on the ships he commanded.

The *Titanic* was almost ready — and a good thing too, since there was less than a week to go. The ship reached Southampton a little after midnight on Friday, April 4. Final preparations began early Friday morning. The ship was loaded with 4,427 tons of coal, adding to the 1,880 tons already on board.

The next day, Saturday, more than three hundred crew members were signed up — bakers, firemen, stewards, window cleaners, butchers, and stewardesses — everything the floating palace needed. Fewer than fifty of the crew were trained seamen, experienced with such things as lowering lifeboats or handling small boats at sea; most were hotel staff, stokers (to keep the furnaces loaded with coal), or engineers.

Captain Edward John Smith of the *Titanic*.

On Monday, trains brought food supplies to G Deck, where they were loaded into storerooms and refrigerators. Although the full list of supplies for the *Titanic* has been lost, we know that her sister ship, the *Olympic*, took on massive quantities of food for a transatlantic voyage. It's likely that the *Titanic* set sail with supplies that included 75,000 pounds of meat; 11,000 pounds of fish; 10,000 pounds of sugar; 36,000 oranges; 7,000 heads of lettuce; 40 tons of potatoes; 40,000 eggs; and 20,000 bottles of beer.

In addition to the supplies for passengers, the *Titanic* was carrying a wide assortment of items. The cargo list included cartons of books; 100 bales of shelled walnuts; 1,196 bags of potatoes; 15 cases of rabbit hair; 63 cases of champagne; plus cheese; brandy; wine; orchids; lace; surgical instruments; feathers for hats; gloves; preserves; mussels; tea; and silk. One passenger was even shipping a red Renault automobile!

❖

Twenty-four-year-old Violet Jessop signed on as a stewardess in the days before sailing. The eldest of six children, Violet had once dreamed of getting an education, but when her mother fell ill, Violet had to help support the family. She followed her mother's path and became a stewardess. Violet was a hard worker and took a lot of pride in caring for "her" passengers, turning down beds at night, bringing tea trays to passengers, and, of course, helping anyone who got seasick.

The layout of the *Titanic* was familiar to Violet, since she had worked on the *Olympic*. The two ships were indeed quite similar, one reason why many of the photographs we see today of the *Titanic*'s interiors are actually of the *Olympic*. However, there were a few differences. One obvious one was that the forward part of the promenade on A Deck on the *Titanic* was enclosed, rather than open. The *Titanic* also had its new restaurant, the Café Parisien, which offered fantastic views of the sea for diners.

The first class Café Parisien on B Deck.

13

Thomas Andrews was the shipbuilder in charge of the design and plans for the *Titanic*.

There were also other, smaller changes. According to Violet, Thomas Andrews, the *Titanic*'s designer, had asked the *Olympic*'s crew for suggestions to improve the new ship and make their long hours at work easier. Violet and her fellow crew members had been eager to contribute ideas for improvements in the stewards' quarters, called "glory holes." On most ships, as Violet knew from her own experience, stewards lived in cramped quarters with little comfort or privacy. The glory hole, Violet wrote, was usually "a foul place, often . . . infected with bugs . . ."

The stewards and stewardesses were delighted with their clean new accommodations on the *Titanic*. Violet found that her bunk was placed the way she had suggested to give her more privacy, and she also had a separate, small wardrobe so that she did not have to share a closet with her roommate. (And since her roommate smoked cigarettes, Violet was pleased that now her own clothes wouldn't smell like smoke!) The crew was so happy they invited Thomas "Tommy" Andrews to visit the glory hole to thank him in person. "His gentle face lit up with real pleasure," Violet remembered fondly.

Thomas Andrews was thirty-nine years old. He had begun working as an apprentice at Harland and Wolff shipbuilders, where his uncle was part owner, when he was only sixteen. Andrews was bright, well liked, dedicated, and hardworking. He probably knew more about the ship than anyone and would be traveling on the *Titanic*'s maiden voyage to take notes and make adjustments. In those last hectic days before sailing, Violet saw his tall frame everywhere. "Often during our rounds we came upon our beloved designer going about unobtrusively with a tired face but a satisfied air."

Thomas Andrews wasn't satisfied unless everything was right. He didn't just walk around giving orders: He rolled up his sleeves and got to work. He even put into place "racks, tables, chairs, berth ladders, and electric fans . . . " his secretary recalled.

"He was always busy, taking the owners around the ship, interviewing engineers, officials, managers, agents, subcontractors . . . and superintending generally the work of completion."

How proud he must have been! For Thomas Andrews, this magnificent ship was the culmination of years of hard work and planning. His last letter to his wife, written on the eve of the maiden voyage, is full of pride and the sense of accomplishment he must have felt. "The *Titanic* is now about complete and will, I think, do the old Firm credit tomorrow when we sail."

Stewardess Violet Jessop was ready too. "Life aboard started off smoothly. Even Jenny, the ship's cat and part of the crew, had immediately picked herself a comfortable corner; she varied her usual Christmas routine on previous ships by presenting *Titanic* with a litter of kittens in April."

But fireman Joe Mulholland, who had worked on the *Titanic* from Belfast to Southampton, said later that he decided not to sign on for the maiden voyage across the Atlantic when he saw Jenny carry her tiny kittens off, one by one, down the gangplank.

He thought it was a bad omen.

❖⟩⟨❖

Even an experienced British seaman like thirty-eight-year-old Second Officer Charles Herbert Lightoller (sometimes known by the nickname "Lights"), who'd worked on White Star ships for twelve years, was impressed by the massive size of the *Titanic*.

"I was thoroughly familiar with pretty well every type of ship afloat, from a battleship and a barge, but it took me fourteen days before I could with confidence find my way from one part of that ship to another by the shortest route," he said.

Getting a new ship ready to sail — especially one that would cater to so many rich and prominent people — took a tremendous amount of effort and attention to small details. Lightoller and the other officers needed to make sure everything was in working order for the voyage. "With the *Titanic* it was night and day work, organizing here, receiving stores there . . ."

But they shared Thomas Andrews's sense of excitement. Everyone could see that the *Titanic* was something special. Lightoller put it this way: "It was clear to everybody on board that we had a ship that was going to create the greatest stir British shipping circles had ever known."

Sailing day arrived at last. It now seemed to Lightoller that the *Titanic* was like a nest of bees about to swarm. Finally, just after noon on Wednesday, April 10, the gangways were lowered, the whistle blew, and the *Titanic* was off!

❧ ❧

As the ship got under way, an eager Frank Browne stood ready, anxious to capture this moment with his camera. He leaned as far over the railing as he dared. "With a feeling akin to suppressed excitement I watched the scene, for it was my first experience of actual travel on an ocean liner, and for a beginning I could not have 'struck' a bigger boat . . ."

The *Titanic* glided out of her berth. Suddenly Frank heard a crack: The wash of the giant ship had caused the ropes holding the ocean liner *New York,* moored nearby, to break. Cut loose, the smaller boat began to drift — right into the *Titanic*'s path.

"A voice beside me said, 'Now for a crash,' and I snapped my shutter," Frank said.

Captain E. J. Smith and the harbor pilot acted quickly to avoid a collision by ordering the engines full astern to keep the great ship from moving forward and break a sort of suction between the ships. Tugs then managed to put lines on the *New York* to pull her away. In the end it took nearly an hour more to get the *Titanic* safely out of the harbor. Before long, though, she was crossing the English Channel to pick up more passengers in Cherbourg, France.

The passengers sat down to enjoy their first meal on board.

⤜⋆⤛

A day later, on Thursday morning at around 11:30 a.m., the *Titanic* lowered her anchor two miles off Cobh harbor, at the Irish port of Queenstown (now called Cobh), to pick up more passengers. It would be the ship's last stop before heading out onto the open seas — and to the New World.

The *Titanic* was too massive for the harbor, so those who were getting on, mostly Irish emigrants in third class, were ferried

Titanic leaves Southampton, England, on April 10, 1912, on her maiden voyage.

WHITE STAR LINE
JAMES SCOTT & Co. Agents.

Telegrams. "ISMAY." Queenstown
Telephone No 3.

Passenger. Department.

Scott's Square,
QUEENSTOWN, April 3rd. 1912.
OLYMPIC. TRIPLE SCREW 45,324 TONS
TITANIC. TRIPLE SCREW. 45000 TONS
THE LARGEST STEAMERS IN THE WORLD

WHITE STAR LINE
SERVICES.

SOUTHAMPTON—CHERBOURG—NEW YORK.
ROYAL & UNITED STATES MAIL STEAMERS.
VIA QUEENSTOWN (WESTBOUND)—PLYMOUTH (EASTBOUND)

LIVERPOOL—NEW YORK.
VIA QUEENSTOWN.

LIVERPOOL—NEW YORK.
(FREIGHT.)

LIVERPOOL—BOSTON.
VIA QUEENSTOWN.

LIVERPOOL—QUEBEC—MONTREAL.

LIVERPOOL—AUSTRALIA.
VIA SOUTH AFRICA.

LIVERPOOL—AUSTRALIA.
(FREIGHT.)

LIVERPOOL—NEW ZEALAND.
(FREIGHT.)

LONDON—NEW ZEALAND.
VIA SOUTH AFRICA.

NEW YORK—MEDITERRANEAN.
VIA AZORES.

BOSTON—MEDITERRANEAN.
VIA AZORES.

THROUGH BOOKINGS
TO ALL PARTS
OF THE WORLD.

Dear Father Browne,   "First Class"
       We have pleasure in handing you
herewith pass from Southampton to Queenstown per
s.s. "Titanic" April 10th, and we trust you will have
an enjoyable trip.

          Yours truly,
          FOR JAMES SCOTT & Co.,

The Rev. F.M. Browne, S.J.
     Bishop's Palace,
          Queenstown.

Frank Browne, a young Irishman who was due to be ordained in 1915 and also known as Father Browne, was given a ticket for passage on the *Titanic*'s maiden voyage, from Southampton, England, to Cork, Ireland, by his uncle.

out to the ship on two tenders, the *America* and the *Ireland*. (Three first class passengers, as well as 113 third class and 7 second class passengers, joined the *Titanic* at Queenstown, along with 1,356 sacks of mail.) Based on extensive study into passenger and crew records, New Zealand researcher Lester Mitcham concludes that overall there were 1,317 passengers on board the *Titanic*: 324 in first class, 284 in second class — including 8 members of the *Titanic*'s band — and 709 in third class. Of these, 522 were women and children.

Letters written during that first day were unloaded in Ireland, and a few passengers got off, including Frank Browne, still holding his camera — along with a packet of exposed photographic glass plates.

Years later, Frank (or Father Frank Browne) recounted that at dinner the first night on board he was befriended by a rich American couple, who offered to pay his way for the entire voyage — all the way to New York. But when he wired his religious order for permission to go, it was denied. The message read: "Get off that ship."

So Frank left the ship — along with his precious photographic plates.

And that's how it happened that today, thanks to Frank Browne and his uncle Robert's generosity, we have his rare, heartbreaking photographs of those first hours of the *Titanic*'s maiden voyage.

21

A couple strolls on the Promenade Deck of the *Titanic*.

Titanic *April 11th*

My dear Mum and Dad
It don't seem possible we are out on the briny writing
to you. Well dears so far we are having a delightful trip
the weather is beautiful and the ship magnificent. We
can't describe the tables it's like a floating town. I can
tell you we do swank we shall miss it on the trains as
we go third on them. You would not imagine you were
on a ship. There is hardly any motion she is so large
we have not felt sick yet we expect to get to
Queenstown today so thought I would drop this
with the mails. . . . . We will post again at New York . . .

Lots of love don't worry about us. Ever your loving
children

Harvey & Lot & Madge

A FLOATING PALACE

Among the letters unloaded at Queenstown was this cheery postcard from Harvey Collyer to his parents back in England. Harvey was a thirty-one-year-old grocery store owner who'd just sold his business in order to bring his family to America. Before the ship set sail, Harvey went to the bank and took out every penny he had — in cash. It came to several thousand dollars.

Harvey, along with his wife, Charlotte, and their eight-year-old daughter, Marjorie, planned to settle in Idaho, where friends were urging them to buy a farm. They hoped the sunnier climate would be good for Charlotte's health, since she suffered from tuberculosis. Harvey was full of all the hopes and dreams of a young father. And what better way to begin a new life than to be sailing on the new, incredible *Titanic*?

Charlotte was also delighted. "The *Titanic* was wonderful, far more splendid and huge than I had dreamed of. The other craft in the harbor were like cockle shells beside her, and they, mind you, were the boats of the American and other lines that a few years ago were thought enormous."

Charlotte wasn't worried about safety; she was sure that even the worst storm couldn't hurt a ship this big. And while she was a bit seasick at first, by Sunday Charlotte felt able to enjoy meals in the dining room. That day the Collyers and other second class passengers enjoyed a hearty lunch menu that included pea soup, spaghetti au gratin, corned beef with vegetable dumplings, roast mutton, as well as an apple tart.

>+<

A woman riding a stationary bicycle in the *Titanic*'s gymnasium. The man in this photo is second class passenger Lawrence Beesley.

A thoughtful young Englishman named Lawrence Beesley was also sailing second class. Lawrence, thirty-four, had resigned his job teaching science to take a long holiday to visit his brother in Canada. His wife, Gertrude, had died in 1906. Lawrence had left his only child, eight-year-old Alec, at home to take this trip.

Before sailing, Lawrence wandered around the ship, astonished by all there was to see. Second class passengers were allowed to tour the first class areas before launch, and Lawrence especially enjoyed peeking into the gymnasium on the starboard side of the Boat Deck.

The gymnasium was an attractive space, about forty-five feet long and seventeen feet wide, with seven arched windows, white walls and ceiling, and three oak columns. The equipment, which might seem rather old-fashioned compared to the high-tech machines of today, included two rowing machines, a stationary bicycle, a weight machine, a device called a "back-massaging machine," and a punchball.

The gymnasium was the domain of a spry, enthusiastic thirty-six-year-old Englishman named Thomas W. McCawley. To Lawrence, the busy instructor seemed the very picture of health, all dressed in white with rosy cheeks and a jaunty mustache. Lawrence watched as McCawley darted here and there, introducing passengers to the latest equipment, "placing one passenger on the electric 'horse,' another on the 'camel,' while the laughing group of onlookers watched the inexperienced riders vigorously shaken up and down as he controlled the little motor which made the machines imitate so realistically horse and camel exercise."

❧•❧

Unlike first-timer Lawrence Beesley, first class passenger Colonel Archibald Gracie was a seasoned transatlantic traveler. An amateur military historian and writer, Colonel Gracie hailed from a wealthy New York family. But even he couldn't help being impressed by the *Titanic*. "I enjoyed myself as if I were in a summer palace on the seashore, surrounded with every comfort — there was nothing to indicate or suggest that we were on the stormy Atlantic."

The ship was certainly designed to please, offering richly decorated public rooms, music concerts, shuffleboard, chess, dominos, card games, cricket, and deck tennis. Some first class passengers stayed in two-bedroom suites with private bathrooms. Others enjoyed staterooms with an extra sitting room, beautiful furniture, wood-paneled walls, and brass or mahogany beds with electric reading lights.

For those passengers who wanted something even more luxurious, the *Titanic* boasted two promenade, or parlor, suites located on B Deck. J. Bruce Ismay, head of the White Star Line, was traveling in one of these.

In addition to having two bedrooms, a private bathroom, and a sitting room, Mr. Ismay's suite had its own enclosed forty-eight-foot-long promenade deck, where he and his guests could relax in deck and lounge chairs. The sitting room was elegant, with rich wood paneling and a carved walnut ceiling. Furniture included a settee, armchairs, a large round table with nine chairs, a writing table, and even a faux (false) fireplace.

A woman named Charlotte Cardeza, traveling with her son and her maid (all later rescued in Lifeboat 3), had booked the

The *Titanic*'s gymnasium. The man in white is the gymnasium steward, Thomas W. McCawley. The gentleman in the background is riding the electrically driven "camel" machine.

A bed in one of the *Titanic*'s many luxury cabins.

other parlor suite. Mrs. Cardeza was traveling with an amazing amount of luggage: "14 trunks, four suitcases, three crates and a medicine chest. Her baggage included 70 dresses, 38 feather boas and 10 fur coats." She also was carrying at least $30,000 in jewelry.

Mrs. Cardeza seems to have been quite a busy woman. She was famous as a yachtswoman and one of the few female big-game hunters of the 1890s! According to the *New York Times*, "In between her game hunting expeditions to Africa and Asia, Mrs. Cardeza twice circumnavigated the world on her yacht."

The wealthy Mrs. Cardeza was right at home on the *Titanic*.

Father Browne's first class stateroom on the *Titanic*.

The *Titanic's* top deck was called the "Boat Deck." It had promenade areas for first class passengers toward the middle of the boat, and for second class passengers in the stern. The lifeboats were stored here. It also contained the captain's bridge, a semi-enclosed cabin with a roof and open side walls. The ship could be steered from here, and also from the Wheelhouse, immediately aft. In addition, the Boat Deck included quarters for the captain and officers, the first class entrance to the grand staircase, and six first class staterooms.

Although the Boat Deck could accommodate forty-eight to sixty-four lifeboats, the *Titanic* was sailing with twenty, of various sizes, which could hold a total of 1,178 people. On her maiden

⇒ WHY WEREN'T THERE ENOUGH LIFEBOATS? ⇐

While the small number of lifeboats seems shocking to us today, it was perfectly legal in 1912. The regulations for lifeboats weren't based on the number of people, but the tonnage of the ship. According to the British Board of Trade, any ship 10,000 gross registered tons and above was required to have sixteen lifeboats. The rules dated back to the Merchant Shipping Act of 1894 and had never been updated to take into account much larger ships like the *Titanic*, which was 46,239 gross registered tons: more than four times the maximum size included in the tables.

voyage, the ship was carrying 2,208 people. (The ship's original designer, Alexander Carlisle, had submitted an early plan for sixty-four lifeboats, which would have been sufficient to rescue all passengers and crew.)

Passengers stroll on the second class deck.

33

❖

First class passengers could also enjoy themselves by strolling on the second highest deck, A Deck, or Promenade Deck, which wasn't open to second or third class passengers. The Promenade Deck was five hundred feet long, on both the starboard and port sides, and the forward part had glass windows to help protect passengers from wind and sea spray. It held chairs, where first class passengers could bundle up with a book, or sit and talk. This deck included first class staterooms and public rooms such as the elegant lounge, with its green and gold carpet, an electric fireplace with a gray marble mantel, and rich oak paneling.

After their stroll on deck, first class passengers could come in through the first class entrance and descend the gorgeous, sweeping grand staircase. This spectacular twenty-foot-wide staircase was accessible from either side of the ship. At the top was the first class entrance hall, designed as a gallery so that passengers could look down onto the grand staircase itself. The entrance hall was more than fifty feet wide, with eleven arched windows. Settees and armchairs were scattered around the hall and a Steinway piano stood on the port side. The white ceiling had decorated wood beams. In the center was an oval dome of magnificent white glass, nineteen by twenty-six feet, decorated with iron and brass work.

The grand staircase itself descended all the way down to D Deck. At the half landing between the Boat Deck and A Deck, the staircase was adorned with a beautiful carved panel, twelve feet high, with a clock in the center. On either side of the clock were two winged figures representing Honor and Glory. A carved oak pedestal with a bronze cherub stood at the foot of the stairs on the A Deck landing. Looking at photographs, it's almost as if one can still hear the rustle of satin dresses and catch the scent of perfume in the air.

Many first class passengers stayed on B Deck, which had ninety-nine first class cabins with room for nearly two hundred people. B Deck also included the second class entrance and foyer, and even a popular elevator to reach cabins on other decks. There was also a second class smoke room with comfortable leather chairs and a bar.

C Deck extended from bow to stern continuously and

The *Titanic*'s grand staircase.

included 135 first class staterooms in the forward section, as well as an enclosed promenade and the library for second class passengers. Aft, there was a general room and smoke room for third class. The enquiry office and purser's office were also on this level. D Deck had accommodations for all classes as well as crew and was the highest level in which second and third class cabins were located. The first class dining saloon was on this level.

All the ship's watertight bulkheads rose as high as the next deck, E Deck, which also included accommodations for all classes (this was the lowest level for any first class cabins). F Deck included more third class cabins than on any other level, along with a large third class dining saloon. G Deck was the lowest level where any passenger cabins were located. It was not continuous and had separate sections. There were third class and crew accommodations forward, along with the post office, a squash racket court, and storage areas. Other parts of the G Deck were taken up with the ship's boilers.

Below G Deck was the Orlop Deck, with sections for cargo holds, the mail room, and machinery. The Tank Top was the lowest level of all, and was like a basement, with its plating forming an inner skin along the bottom of the ship.

❖

The *Titanic* has been described as several small towns — one for each class. It boasted an amazing array of food service options, from separate dining rooms for each class to several additional restaurants for first class passengers. The meals, especially in first class, rivaled the dinners in a fine restaurant onshore. First class passengers ate on bone china, some edged in twenty-two karat gold.

To reach the first class dining saloon, passengers could descend the grand staircase to a lovely reception room on D Deck, which served as a central meeting place and boasted tables as well as comfortable sofas and chairs. From this richly carpeted room, doors led into the dining room. This is where most first class passengers ate, since the cost of meals was included in their tickets.

The menu in the first class dining room was designed to cater to passengers accustomed to fine dining: People could enjoy such delicacies as oysters, poached salmon, roast duckling, lamb with mint sauce, and sirloin steak, with éclairs, pastries, or apple meringue for dessert.

37

➨◅

While the grown-ups enjoyed the meals, ocean views, and accommodations, nine-year-old Frankie Goldsmith, traveling in third class, was happy just to have an exciting new playground to explore.

Frankie's family had been talking for months about going to America to join his aunt Eliza and her family, who lived near Detroit, Michigan. It had been a hard winter for Frankie and his parents. Frankie's baby brother, Albert, had died of diphtheria just a few months before. Spring seemed the right time for a fresh start, and the young family made a fateful decision — they would leave their home and friends for a new life.

First class passengers on White Star Line's Olympic-class ships enjoyed luxurious dining experiences (above). A first class dinner menu (right).

R.M.S. "TITANIC"
APRIL 14, 1912

FIRST CLASS DINNER

HORS D'OEUVRE VARIES

OYSTERS

CONSOMME OLGA   CREAM OF BARLEY

SALMON, MOUSSELINE SAUCE, CUCUMBER

FILET MIGNONS LILI

SAUTE OF CHICKEN LYONNAISE

VEGETABLE MARROW FARCIE

LAMB, MINT SAUCE

ROAST DUCKLING, APPLE SAUCE

SIRLOIN OF BEEF   CHATEAU POTATOES

GREEN PEAS   CREAMED CARROTS

BOILED RICE

PARMENTIER & BOILED NEW POTATOES

PUNCH ROMAINE

ROAST SQUAB & CRESS

RED BURGUNDY

COLD ASPARAGUS   VINAIGRETTE

PATE DE FOIE GRAS

CELERY

WALDORF PUDDING

PEACHES IN CHARTREUSE JELLY

CHOCOLATE & VANILLA ECLAIRS

FRENCH ICE CREAM

Frankie's father had saved diligently for the voyage. On the day the *Titanic* set sail, Frankie and his parents, along with a friend, Thomas Theobald, took the train to London. There they picked up Alfred Rush, a teenager whom they'd promised to escort safely to friends in Detroit.

The traveling companions took the early boat train to Southampton with other second and third class passengers. Once on board the ship, a steward helped Frankie and his parents find their private third class cabin. Since most people traveled second and third class, these passengers were scheduled to arrive on board earlier to allow more time for families to find their cabins on D, E, F, or G deck; store their luggage; and settle crying babies.

If Frankie Goldsmith's cabin was not as fancy as one in first or second class, he certainly wouldn't have noticed. Frankie was too busy running around with his new friends, a gang of seven or eight boys around his own age.

Two of his friends were probably fellow third class passengers Rossmore and Eugene Abbott, ages sixteen and thirteen, returning to America with their mother, Rhoda, who became acquainted with Frankie's mother on board.

Soon after leaving Ireland, the boys decided to try to climb up one of the cargo cranes used for lifting heavy items onto the ship, located on the Poop Deck, which was the third class promenade area in the stern. Of course Frankie went first. It would be like climbing trees back home. There was only one problem: When Frankie tried to grip the cable, he discovered it was covered in grease to protect it from the salty air.

40

Frankie hung on with all his might. It didn't help that a group of sailors nearby burst into laughter at his predicament. It also didn't help that his mother was *not* exactly happy at seeing his greasy hands and made him scrub them until at last they were clean — and probably bright red!

⇛ ⇚

Third class passengers like Frankie and his friends were restricted to their own areas, partly by custom and also because of the separation of immigrants required by United States Immigration. But while there were clearly marked areas and evidence of gates, a researcher notes that "one myth that persists to this day is that of locked gates extending from floor-to-ceiling between the third class areas and the rest of the ship. It must be noted that there is no evidence, either documented or from the wreck, that any such barriers existed . . ."

41

But Frankie and his friends were less interested in fancy first class rooms than in wandering around E Deck. Here, doors from the boilers opened onto an alleyway called "Scotland Road," the main walkway fore and aft used by third class passengers.

Frankie liked to watch the "black gang," so called because their faces and arms were usually coated with coal dust. These were the firemen, trimmers, and greasers who worked in the *Titanic*'s six boiler rooms down in the Tank Top, where the ship's twenty-nine massive boilers (each more than fifteen feet high) were located.

"We young boys also spent a lot of time peering down into the ship's steam boiler rooms watching the stokers and firemen at work," said Frankie. ". . . They were singing songs, often, while

The immense funnels of a White Star Line's Olympic-class ship.

we looked down at them, some of them rattling their coal shovels on the grates of the coal burners . . ."

Greasers assisted in the engine room, oiling and greasing the turning equipment. Each fireman usually tended three furnaces, loading in the coal to keep the fires steady. (Firemen and stokers both shoveled coal, but according to leading stoker Frederick Barrett, the position of a stoker was considered more important, or "a little higher," than a fireman.) Trimmers cooled the ash removed from the boilers with a hose. They also moved coal close to the boilers to keep the supply full. The boiler rooms were supervised by an engineer.

The black gang had to shovel all the coal by hand into the *Titanic*'s 159 furnaces, which consumed about 650 tons of coal a day. The coal-fired furnaces heated water in the boilers. This generated steam, which was forced into the engine to create the power needed to turn the propellers. The exhaust smoke vented through three of the *Titanic*'s gigantic funnels.

43

These funnels stood over 60 feet above the Boat Deck. The distance from their tops down to the bottom of the keel was nearly three times that — 175 feet. The *Titanic* had four funnels: The fourth was used primarily for ventilation, but it definitely made the ship look more impressive.

Thanks to the hard work of the men of the black gang, the *Titanic* was making excellent time on her maiden voyage. The seas were calm and the sky clear. As the morning of Sunday, April 14, dawned, it seemed certain that the magnificent ship would have no trouble making New York harbor by Wednesday morning — right on schedule.

The Promenade Deck.

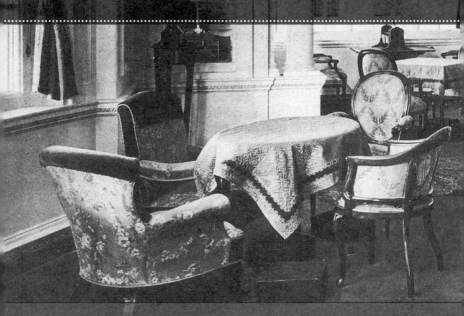

On board RMS Titanic, *Sunday afternoon*

My dear ones all,
As you see it is Sunday afternoon & we are reading in the Library after luncheon . . . Well the sailors say we have had a wonderful passage up to now. . . . . This mighty expanse of water, no land in sight & the ship rolling from side to side is very wonderful tho they say this ship does not roll on account of its size. Any how it rolls enough for me . . . . it is nice weather but awfully windy & cold. . . . .

From your loving Esther

The *Titanic*'s first class reading and writing room looked much like this one on the *Olympic.*

CHAPTER THREE
A PEACEFUL SUNDAY

Jack Thayer was a smart and sophisticated young American. He might have been too old for climbing cables like young Frankie Goldsmith, but as he said later, "being seventeen years old, I was all over the ship."

Jack was traveling first class with his father, John B. Thayer, vice president of the Pennsylvania Railroad, and his mother, Marian, who'd just been shopping in Paris. His mother's maid, Margaret Fleming, completed the party.

Young Jack had a bright future ahead of him. He planned to graduate from high school in the spring, enter Princeton University, and embark on a career in banking. "It was planned. It was a certainty," he wrote later.

But as Jack learned that night, nothing in life is truly certain.

Jack spent most of Sunday walking the promenade decks with his parents and chatting with friends and acquaintances. As the afternoon went on, he realized the weather was getting colder. So it wasn't a surprise when he heard that the ship had received ice warnings and might be entering ice fields later on that night. J. Bruce Ismay, who had been given one of these warnings by the captain, was sharing it with passengers.

"I remember Mr. Ismay showing us a wire regarding the presence of ice and remarking that we would not reach that position until around nine p.m.," Jack said.

That evening, Jack's parents were invited to a dinner honoring Captain Smith, so Jack ate alone at their regular table. Over after-dinner coffee, he met a young man named Milton

47

Long. In a letter to Milton's parents after the disaster, Jack told them about how he got acquainted with their only son.

"I was sitting in the room outside the main dining saloon, waiting for the music to begin. I had dined alone and was sitting alone, my father and mother having been invited out to dine in the restaurant . . . Your son was sitting in front and to one side of us, with his back toward me. He took out a cigarette and having no matches, came up to my table and asked if he might take a match . . .

"He looked lonely, sitting all alone, and I was lonely, so I pulled my chair up to his table and asked if I might join him. He smiled and said, 'Yes, certainly.' . . . We talked about cricket and baseball . . . He told me of his trip around the world and of getting shipwrecked in Alaska . . . We talked for about two hours and a half together. Then I saw mother and father come downstairs, so I said goodnight to your son."

Having agreed to meet Milton again the next day, Jack got ready to turn in for the night. But first, he put on his overcoat and took one more stroll on deck to gaze at the stars. The memory of that beautiful night stayed with him.

"It had become very much colder. It was a brilliant, starry night," he said. "There was no moon and I have never seen the stars shine brighter; they appeared to stand right out of the sky, sparkling like cut diamonds."

⋙⋘

By Sunday morning, first class passenger Colonel Archibald Gracie figured he had slacked off his usual exercise routines long enough. He prided himself on being a fit fifty-three. But since the *Titanic* sailed, he had spent his time playing cards, eating fine food, and chatting with acquaintances such as his old friend James Clinch Smith, a popular member of New York society, who'd been living in Paris with his wife, Bertha. Clinch Smith returned to America once each year, and Gracie was glad to have this time to catch up.

Still, now it was time for some discipline, so Gracie headed for the gymnasium. "I was up early before breakfast and met the professional racquet player in a half hour's warming up," he said. Then he headed to F Deck, to the *Titanic*'s pool, for "a swim in the six-foot deep tank of salt water, heated to a refreshing temperature."

Passengers on cruise ships today expect features such as swimming pools, but when the *Titanic* was built, this was a new luxury. In fact, the *Titanic* and the *Olympic* were two of the first ships to offer a swimming pool, called the "swimming bath," which was reserved for first class passengers. First class men could use the swimming bath for free from six until nine each morning, after which there was a small fee of twenty-five cents. Ladies had use of the bath from ten a.m. until one p.m.

The swimming bath itself was thirty-three feet long and fourteen feet wide. It was about seven feet six inches deep at the forward end and eight feet four inches deep at the aft end, although the water was apparently never filled all the way. There weren't any diving boards either. Although the *Olympic* had been fitted with springboards, these turned out to be too dangerous at sea. People could slip and lose their balance easily, and besides, the water sloshed around a lot even if the ship was pitching only slightly.

49

Near the pool was a row of thirteen dressing cubicles with mahogany doors. There were also separate showers decorated with ceramic tiles. The room itself was covered in blue and white ceramic tiles and was located near another popular onboard attraction, the Turkish Baths.

All that exercise made Colonel Gracie hungry. After a hearty breakfast, he attended church service and spent a pleasant day reading and chatting with fellow passengers. He had dinner with several friends, including James Clinch Smith. He and Clinch Smith enjoyed their coffee while listening to the *Titanic*'s band. But Gracie decided not to stay up too late talking or playing cards. He wanted to be up in the morning to exercise again.

Colonel Gracie went to bed early. He would be very glad that he did.

52

⇒⃗⃖

Frankie Goldsmith went to church service that Sunday with his mother. Afterward, they noticed that their traveling companion, Alfred Rush, nicknamed "Alfie," was wanted in the purser's office. (On board ships, the purser was a little like a hotel manager or clerk, who handled money and supplies and kept the passengers' accounts.)

Alfie found them again a short time later. With a wide grin, he held up a six-penny piece. It was an unexpected refund: He'd paid more than needed for his baggage.

"'Look, Mrs. Goldsmith! I've got a birthday present!'" he cried excitedly. "'Frankie, I am sixteen-years old today. Look, I am wearing my long trousers.'"

To Alfie, it was a milestone birthday: Wearing long trousers was a symbol of being a man.

❦

Meanwhile, science teacher Lawrence Beesley spent a peaceful Sunday afternoon in the second class library. It was a clear day, and people were excited about landing in New York on Wednesday, with calm weather all the way.

After dinner, Lawrence and about a hundred other passengers gathered around a piano in the second class dining saloon to sing hymns. Reverend Ernest Carter, who organized the gathering, closed the evening by saying that this was "the first time that there have been hymns sung on this boat on a Sunday evening, but we trust and pray it won't be the last." It was after ten o'clock when they stopped to enjoy some biscuits and coffee. Then Lawrence headed to his cabin on D Deck (D56), to read in his bunk before going to sleep.

❦

On Sunday night the sky was bright with stars, and the first class dining saloon glittered too. May Futrelle was traveling with her husband, Jacques, a writer. She never forgot Sunday night's dinner in the elegant saloon, when many women wore the fine dresses they'd just purchased in Paris.

"It was a brilliant crowd. Jewels flashed from the gowns of the women," May said later. "And, oh, the dear women, how fondly they wore their latest Parisian gowns! It was the first time that most of them had an opportunity to display their newly acquired finery."

The first class dining room.

It didn't seem at all as if they were in the middle of the North Atlantic, May reflected. Instead, she imagined herself in a magnificent New York City hotel. And no wonder. The first class dining saloon could seat more than 550 people — it was the largest dining room on board any ship afloat at the time, 113 feet long and reaching across the full width of the *Titanic*. The walls and ceiling were a glowing white, the furniture oak, and the room sparkled, thanks to the lights of more than 400 bulbs. Chairs at the 115 tables were adorned with pale green leather and had special pegs to help keep them steady in high seas.

In those days, people dressed in formal dinner attire. Dinner started at seven p.m. and was announced by a bugle call. Crystal and china adorned the tables. "I remember at our table there was a great bunch of American beauty roses," May said. "We were all filled with the joy of living. . . ."

56

After dinner May stepped out on deck to take in the beauty of the night. She didn't stay long; it was much colder than she had expected. "There was death chill in the air which sent a shudder through me and caused me to hurry back into the cheer and warmth of the cabin. . . ."

>>• •<<

That dark, clear night drew many people outside for a last look at the stars before bed. Even a seasoned traveler like stewardess Violet Jessop slipped out on deck for a few moments after her duties were done.

"It was all so quiet, but how penetratingly cold it had become! Little wisps of mist like tiny fairies wafted gently inboard from the sea and left my face clammy. I shivered," said Violet.

"It was indeed a night for bed, warmth, and cozy thoughts of home and firesides. I thought of the man in the crow's nest as I came indoors, surely an unenviable job on such a night."

Since she had served on other ships, Violet knew that lookouts were posted twenty-four hours a day in the crow's nest high above the deck. But since the introduction of Guglielmo Marconi's new wireless system, first demonstrated in 1896, ships like the *Titanic* also had another way to learn about what lay ahead. Like the ship itself, the Marconi system was a symbol of a new century of progress.

Both of the *Titanic*'s wireless operators had been trained at the Marconi school in Liverpool, England. Lead operator Jack Phillips, though only twenty-four, had been working as an operator for six years. Harold Bride, twenty-two, who'd begun the previous July, had already completed several transatlantic round-trips. Rather than working for the White Star Line, the radio operators were employed by the Marconi Communication Company Limited.

Phillips and Bride had been trained to operate the Marconi wireless apparatus, which could transmit messages for at least 250 miles, and even farther at night under good conditions. The equipment was so new that the two young men had just unpacked it the week before.

Jack Phillips and Harold Bride spent most of their time sending and receiving telegraphic signals, called "Marconigrams." The majority were private, personal messages from passengers to family and friends, which were sent using Morse code over the Marconi apparatus. Messages were sent to a relay, or shore station, at Cape Race in Newfoundland, Canada. From there

57

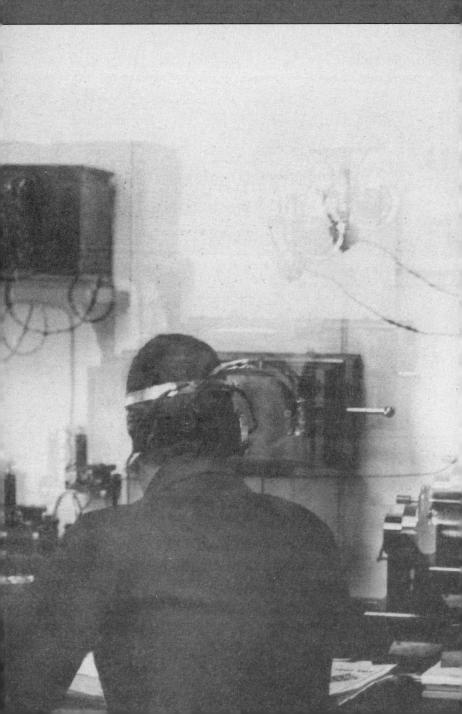

Wireless operator Harold Bride at work in the Marconi Room of the *Titanic*.

messages could be relayed to other shore stations to friends and family on the eastern seaboard and beyond. For passengers, sending a Marconigram was a little like sending a text message while on vacation today. But the process then was a lot more time-consuming. Passengers could write out messages by hand and pay for them at the enquiry office. Messages were then sent by a pneumatic tube to the wireless cabin. Incoming messages were written down by hand by the operator who received them, then typed up by the relief officer and sent by tube back to the enquiry office, where bellboys would pick them up and deliver them to passengers.

These personal messages kept Jack and Harold busy (and also made money for the Marconi company). Ships also relayed messages back and forth to one another. "The *Titanic* herself acted as a relay for messages from vessels lacking sufficient transmitter range to reach the north American coast direct, putting the *Titanic*'s operators in regular contact with fellow operators on nearby ships. Alongside messages from passengers were navigational signals, to be passed on by the Marconi operator to the captain."

The operators handled messages from many ships in the North Atlantic that had been sending the *Titanic* messages of congratulations on her maiden voyage. Messages were addressed to the *Titanic*'s call letters: MGY.

Last but not least were messages from other ships about conditions at sea. These would turn out to be the most important of all — warnings of ice ahead.

At nine o'clock on Sunday morning, the *Caronia*, eastbound from New York, sent the *Titanic* a message with the heading MSG.

59

This meant that it was a Master's Service Gram, from one captain to another. From their training, Jack Phillips and Harold Bride knew that messages marked MSG always had to be delivered to the bridge. That was the rule, and they followed it precisely.

Captain Smith posted this one on the notice board for the officers to see: "Captain, *Titanic* — West-bound steamers report bergs, growlers and field ice in 42° N, from 49° to 51° W, April 12, Compliments, Barr."

This message showed that the ice was directly in the path of the *Titanic*.

⇒►◄⇐

Captain Smith received a similar message from the *Baltic* in the early afternoon, which he passed along to J. Bruce Ismay, who showed it to some of the passengers, including Jack Thayer and his parents. Ismay didn't appear to be worried by the warnings. Around seven o'clock on Sunday evening Captain Smith took the message back from Ismay and sent it to the bridge to post.

But not every warning reached the bridge. One message, from the *Amerika* at 1:45 p.m., noted that the ship had passed two large icebergs. But, since it wasn't marked MSG, it didn't require the radio operators to deliver it to the bridge. For one reason or another, it never made it.

Another message, at 7:30 p.m., from the *Californian* to the *Antillian*, was overheard by the *Titanic*. In it, the *Californian* reported seeing three large icebergs. Harold Bride remembered taking it to the bridge and handing it to an officer, though he did not recall who it was.

These warnings from other ships crossing the Atlantic all told the same story: The *Titanic* was about to enter an area of ice.

❖

A little before nine o'clock on Sunday evening, Captain Smith excused himself from dinner with Jack Thayer's parents and other first class passengers to return to the bridge, where he checked in with Second Officer Charles Herbert Lightoller.

As Lightoller remembered it, he and the captain stood for a while talking about the weather and the sea conditions. It had grown very cold — only one degree above freezing. But what surprised them most on that night in the North Atlantic was the unusually flat, calm sea.

Lightoller said later, "In my fifteen years' experience on the Atlantic I had certainly never seen anything like it . . .

61

"I said something about it was rather a pity the breeze had not kept up whilst we were going through the ice region. Of course, my reason was obvious; he knew I meant the water ripples breaking on the base of the berg," Lightoller told investigators.

Both officers knew that without a breeze to create ripples, icebergs would be harder to see.

"In the event of meeting ice there are many things we look for," Lightoller testified after the disaster. "In the first place a slight breeze. Of course, the stronger the breeze the more visible will the ice be, or rather the breakers on the ice.

"Therefore at any time when there is a slight breeze you will always see at nighttime a phosphorescent line round a berg, growler, or whatever it may be; the slight swell which we invariably look for in the North Atlantic causes the same effect, the break on the base of the berg, so showing a phosphorescent glow."

A growler, as Lightoller explained, is "really the worst form of ice. It is a larger berg melted down, or I might say a solid body of ice which is lower down to the water. . . ." This would make it more difficult to see than a large iceberg.

Still, as they gazed out at the calm seas ahead, Captain Smith and Lightoller decided that even without breakers to mark the location of ice, they would be able to see a certain amount of reflected light from an iceberg — surely enough light to spot anything dangerous in time.

➤‧◄

62

Captain Smith was relying on his long experience. After all, he had crossed the Atlantic many times safely. He'd once told the *New York Times*: ". . . when anyone asks me how I can best describe my experience in nearly 40 years at sea, I merely say uneventful. Of course there have been winter gales, and storms and fog and the like, but in all my experience, I have never been in any accident of any sort worth speaking about."

Earlier, around 5:50 p.m., Captain Smith had called for an alteration in course to South 86° West, slightly to the south and west of the normal route. The ship's course called for a change in direction at a certain spot in the ocean, which was called "turning the Corner," to follow a more direct westward course heading toward Nantucket, off the coast of Massachusetts.

But this precaution would not necessarily be very effective, as the *Titanic* was still far enough north that she would remain in the area of ice. In other words, Captain Smith seemed confident — in hindsight, overly confident — that if any iceberg large enough to cause any damage appeared, the lookouts and the officers on the bridge would be able to see it in time.

And so Captain Smith left the bridge about 9:25 p.m., saying to Lightoller, "'If it becomes at all doubtful let me know at once; I will be just inside.'"

63

> *In latitude 42 N. to 41.25, longitude 49 W. to longitude 50.30 W., saw much heavy pack ice and great number large icebergs, also field ice, weather good, clear.*
>
> — *Mesaba* to *Titanic*, April 14, 1912, 9:40 p.m.

A distant photograph of the iceberg that is claimed to have sunk the *Titanic*.

"ICEBERG RIGHT AHEAD."

The night kept getting colder.

On the bridge, Second Officer Lightoller knew the ship would be entering an area of ice soon. Just after the captain left, he asked James Moody, the junior officer on duty, to call the crow's nest. Lightoller gave instructions for Moody to pass on: He wanted the men to keep a sharp lookout throughout the night for ice, particularly small ice and growlers.

At 9:40 p.m., twenty minutes before the watch changed at 10 p.m., a message came into the radio room from a ship called the *Mesaba* warning of heavy pack ice and large icebergs. Where? Right ahead of the *Titanic*.

Yet this message didn't contain the prefix MSG, marking it a priority message from captain to captain. Harold Bride was off duty, taking a nap. Both operators were still trying to catch up on their sleep — they'd been up most of Friday night repairing their equipment. Jack Phillips was swamped with passenger messages.

For all these reasons, somehow the warning from the *Mesaba* just didn't make it to the bridge.

Lightoller said later, "The wireless operator was not to know how close we were to this position, and therefore the extreme urgency of the message."

Would getting that message have made a difference in what happened that night? Maybe. But maybe not.

After all, the ship had already received several warnings. And still the captain hadn't put additional lookouts into place.

DEUTSCHE BETR... B...
FÜR DRAHTLOSE ...EL...

Quittung №				DEUTSCHE BET...
Bordgebühren:		Mk.	Pf.	FÜR DRAHTLOS...
Küsten				Berlin S.W.
Land		1.05		
Sonstige				Radio
Zusammen		1. Mk 05	Pf.	Station
Sende Nr.	5	mit 22	W.	1912 den 14/4

Genaue Adresse, deutliche Handschrift. — State exact address, write distinctly. — P...

Hydrogra...

Amerika passed

in 41° 27 N 50°

Zur Beachtung. Die Deutsch Betriebsgsellschaft fü...
der durch Nichtübermittelung, Verstümmelung, Verzögeru...

ESELLSCHAFT
RAFIE M. B. H.

SGESELLSCHAFT
EGRAFIE M. B. H.
hofer Ufer 9.

gramm

Lfd. № 110

Befördert den 14 4 1912

11 Uhr 45 Min am

en D. „Titanic"

durch Reuter

Charakter M X G

via Cape Race

11 Uhr 20 Minuten am

ire l'adresse exactement et lisiblement. — Se ruega dirección exacta y escritura leíble.

c Office Washington DC

vo large icebergs.

W on the 14th of April

Knuth

lose Telegrafie m. b. H., Berlin, ist nicht haftbar für einen Schaden
ler Bestellung usw. des Telegramms entstehen kann.

A radio telegram from the German ship *Amerika* to the *Titanic*, warning the crew of icebergs.

Nor had he given an order for the ship to go slower — even though a ship as large as the *Titanic* was not easy to turn.

Walter Lord, author of *A Night to Remember*, the most famous book about the *Titanic*, put it this way: "Above all, the cumulative effect of the messages — warning after warning, the whole day long — was lost completely. The result was a complacency, an almost arrogant casualness, that permeated the bridge."

Ten o'clock came.

Lightoller handed the watch over to First Officer William M. Murdoch. The ship continued to steam full speed ahead — about 22½ knots (a knot is equivalent to 6,076 feet or 1.151 miles an hour).

In the crow's nest, lookouts Reginald Lee and Frederick Fleet arrived to relieve George Symons and Archie Jewell. Symons and Jewell passed on the orders from Lightoller: Keep a sharp lookout for small ice and growlers.

"All right," replied Frederick Fleet. At twenty-four, he had already had four years' experience as a lookout on the *Oceanic* before joining the *Titanic*.

As seven bells (11:30 p.m.) rang, it was still cold, clear, and calm. Most of the men, women, and children on the *Titanic* had turned in for the night, lulled by the now-familiar hum of the engines. About this time Frederick Fleet said he noticed "a sort of slight haze." Along with the calm, flat sea, a haze could make spotting ice even more difficult.

Then, just before 11:40 p.m., Fleet spied what looked to him like a dark mass straight ahead. It appeared to be directly in the *Titanic*'s path. Fleet sounded the warning bell with three sharp rings and telephoned down to the bridge: "'Iceberg right ahead.'"

Sixth Officer Moody picked up the phone. "'Thank you,'" he answered, and hung up.

"I reported it as soon as ever I seen it," Fleet testified later. "I reported an iceberg right ahead."

It had seemed small when he first spotted it — maybe the size of two tables put together. But it soon loomed larger, a dark shape rising high above the calm surface of the sea.

On the bridge, First Officer William Murdoch, an experienced seaman, had probably already spotted the shape on his own. He went into action.

Each second was critical, and there wouldn't be many of them. The exact sequence of what happened next — or should have happened — is still unclear.

One thing is certain, though. Murdoch had little time and few good options.

⇒·⇐

Murdoch didn't want to hit the iceberg full on. The ship's bow would probably have been crushed in a head-on collision. And it's likely the accident would have resulted in severe injuries and even death to some passengers and crew. It's possible that with the damage from a head-on collision the *Titanic* might have remained afloat long enough for rescue ships to arrive. But Murdoch couldn't know what would happen. And no seaman deliberately crashes a ship.

So Murdoch did what he could to try to avoid an accident. He would try to steer around the iceberg, hoping that the damage, if there was any, would be less serious than a head-on collision. It wouldn't be easy. After all, the *Titanic* was a 46,000-ton object moving at 38 feet a second.

The *Titanic* was probably only about three ship lengths from the iceberg when Murdoch gave his first order. He aimed to turn the ship to the left as quickly as possible to avoid a direct hit. Fourth Officer Boxhall testified, "I heard the first Officer give the order, 'Hard-a-starboard,' and I heard the engine room telegraph bells ringing."

Sixth Officer Moody, standing behind quartermaster Robert Hichens at the ship's wheel, repeated the instruction. Hichens carried it out, turning the wheel hard over. Murdoch also ordered astern full, probably on the starboard engine.

Fred Barrett, a stoker in Boiler Room 6, the most forward of the ship's boiler rooms, was surprised to suddenly see a red light flash. He knew this was the signal to start closing the dampers to shut off the engines. But what he couldn't figure out was why he was being ordered to stop the engines now — on such a calm, clear night.

Meanwhile, up on the bridge, the flurry of activity continued, with everything seeming to happen at once.

Murdoch quickly activated the switch to close the ship's automatic watertight doors in the compartments below to help contain any flooding. The stern of the great ship swung close to the iceberg. At some point Murdoch probably also ordered "hard-a-port" to try to maneuver around the berg. As researcher David G. Brown has noted, "Murdoch's hard-a-port order would have swung the stern away from the bow." In this way, Murdoch was able to limit the damage to the bow.

Murdoch tried his best. He had so little time.

The seconds ticked by. Thirty-seven seconds in all.

They were not enough.

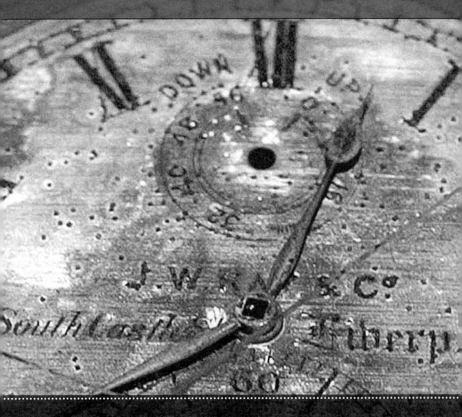

A chronometer from the bridge of the *Titanic*, which was raised from the wreck of the ship.

"It was not a loud crash; it was felt almost as much as heard. . . . I sat up in bed and looked out of the nearest port. I saw an iceberg only a few feet away, apparently racing aft at high speed and crumbling as it went. I knew right away what that meant."
— Henry Harper, first class passenger

IMPACT!

11:40 p.m. Collision!

Quartermaster Alfred Olliver was walking onto the bridge when he heard a "long, grinding sound."

In the crow's nest, the iceberg seemed like "a great, big mass" to lookout Frederick Fleet. Beside him, Reginald Lee watched it approach through the haze, all dark with only a "white fringe" along the top. As the iceberg passed he saw that the back of it appeared white.

Captain Smith was on the bridge in a flash. He got Murdoch's report and together they used the regular and emergency telegraph to send an ALL STOP signal to the engine room.

At the moment of impact, fireman George Beauchamp, down below in Boiler Room 6, was startled by a noise like thunder. He'd just heard stoker Fred Barrett shout, "Shut the dampers!" Closing the dampers on the furnaces was part of the process of stopping the engines.

Cold ocean water began leaking in from gashes in the hull about two feet above the deck. Seconds later, Fred Barrett and second engineer James Hesketh raced out of Boiler Room 6, back toward Boiler Room 5. The watertight door between the two boiler rooms, which Murdoch had closed from the bridge, slammed down shut behind them. George Beauchamp continued to work — for perhaps as long as twenty minutes — before he and other firemen scrambled up an escape ladder to get out of the steam-filled room, with water still pouring in.

73

At 11:41 p.m. the *Titanic*'s engines stopped for the first time.

Captain Smith and Murdoch walked back along the starboard side of the bridge to try to catch a glimpse of the iceberg as it receded in the distance. Fourth Officer Joseph Boxhall tagged along, but he couldn't spot the berg.

Captain Smith sent Boxhall off to do a quick inspection. Boxhall hurried down to the third class passenger accommodations forward on F Deck, looking for damage.

⇒⁂⇐

Awakened by the collision, White Star Line managing director J. Bruce Ismay didn't stop to dress. Throwing a coat over his pajamas, he made his way to the bridge right away to talk to Captain Smith. The two stood together for several minutes, but no one heard what they said.

Then, at 11:47 p.m., Captain Smith ordered the engines to start up "half ahead."

It's not certain what he had in mind. He didn't have damage reports in yet. So why start moving again? Some people think he and Ismay may have discussed heading for Halifax, Nova Scotia, which was closer than New York. Maybe the two men hoped the ship could somehow limp into harbor safely. But that was not to be.

Meanwhile, Boxhall returned with good news. He'd seen "no damage whatever . . ." Captain Smith must have been relieved — at least for a few minutes. But it was a large ship and he needed more information. Boxhall testified later that the captain sent him off again, this time to find the carpenter to check, or "sound," the ship.

Marconi wireless operators on board ships of the time worked long hours transmitting messages from passengers to friends and family onshore.

In the Marconi room, Harold Bride, the *Titanic*'s junior wireless operator, had just woken up. He wasn't aware of the commotion or even the collision itself. "I didn't even feel the shock . . ." Bride said. "There was no jolt whatever."

Bride was trying to convince senior operator Jack Phillips to get some rest when Captain Smith stuck his head into the wireless cabin. Bride remembered it this way:

"'We've struck an iceberg,' the Captain said, 'and I'm having an inspection made to tell what it has done for us. You better get ready to send out a call for assistance. But don't send it until I tell you.'"

Captain Smith soon found out that Boxhall's report was too good to be true. Boxhall had gone only to F Deck. But the damage was in the lowest level of the ship, where the cargo holds and boiler rooms were located.

Sent to find the carpenter, Boxhall ran into him at A Deck, "absolutely out of breath." Carpenter John Hutchinson was already hurrying to the bridge to report bad news: The ship was making water fast. Boxhall also met a mail clerk hurrying to the bridge to tell the captain that the mail hold was filling with seawater.

Six minutes earlier, Captain Smith had ordered the engines half ahead.

Now, at 11:53 p.m., he couldn't ignore the serious reports he was getting. He gave the command for ALL STOP.

Then it was time to investigate for himself.

⤜⤛

While Captain Smith was trying frantically to find out just how badly the ship was damaged, many on board were barely aware that anything was wrong.

When the ship struck the iceberg, Lawrence Beesley was in his cabin, curled up with a book. At first the only thing he was aware of was "an extra heave" of the engines. "Nothing more than that — no sound of a crash or of anything else," he said, "no sense of shock, no jar that felt like one heavy body meeting another. . . ."

Lawrence went back to reading. Then the engines stopped.

Now that made him curious. He wondered if the ship had dropped a propeller. Since this was his first time at sea, Lawrence was interested in everything that went on. Why not go exploring? He threw a dressing gown over his pajamas and pulled on his shoes.

In the corridor he spotted a steward and asked why the ship had stopped. The answer the steward gave him was similar to what many passengers first heard: " 'I don't suppose it is anything much.' "

Lawrence wasn't worried either at this point. How could anything really be wrong with the massive, magnificent ship on such a clear, still night? In fact, he began to feel a bit foolish roaming around the ship in his dressing gown. He didn't see anyone else at first, and it *was* awfully cold.

Still, curiosity got the better of him and he kept on with his wanderings, making his way up to the Boat Deck. Outside, the bitter cold cut him like a knife.

Once again, nothing seemed to be wrong. It was cold

77

and clear — no iceberg or other ship in sight. Beesley went down to the first class smoke room on A Deck, where some fellow passengers had an answer for him: Yes, they'd seen an iceberg go by. But, no, they certainly weren't taking *that* very seriously.

"'I expect the iceberg has scratched off some of her new paint,' said one, 'and the captain doesn't like to go on until she is painted up again.'"

The joking continued. Another man held out his glass of whiskey and laughed, "'Just run along the deck and see if any ice has come aboard: I would like some for this.'"

Then Lawrence noticed that the ship had started again, "moving very slowly through the water with a little white line of foam on either side. I think we were all glad to see this: it seemed better than standing still."

Reassured that they were once again on their way, the young teacher turned to go back to his cabin, book, and warm bed. After all, it must be some minor problem; nothing to worry about. But as he headed down the stairs to his cabin he saw something that made him stop in his tracks: The ship seemed just slightly tilted lower toward the bow, or front end.

He began walking down the steps, a little more worried now. It was hard to describe, but something was definitely wrong. He had "a curious sense of something out of balance and not being able to put one's feet down in the right place."

Lawrence went back to his cabin and his book. It wouldn't be for long.

On the bridge, Captain Smith stopped at the Marconi room on his way to inspect the ship to order the wireless operators to send the international call for assistance: CQD.

Harold Bride tried to make light of what was happening. "I cut in with a little remark that made us all laugh, including the Captain," said Harold. "'Send S.O.S.,' I said. 'It's the new call, and it may be your last chance to send it.'"

With a laugh, Jack Phillips changed the CQD call to SOS.

⇒·⇐

Second class passenger Charlotte Collyer had turned into her berth early, her eight-year-old daughter, Marjorie, beside her. Her husband, Harvey, came into the cabin later and the two chatted as he got ready for bed. Charlotte definitely felt the collision when it happened.

"The sensation to me was as if the ship had been seized by a giant hand and shaken once, twice then stopped dead in its course," she said. But ". . . I was not thrown out of my berth, and my husband staggered on his feet only slightly. We heard no strange sounds . . . but we noticed that the engines had stopped running . . ."

Harvey decided to investigate. Charlotte waited for him sleepily in the warm bunk, curled up with Marjorie. She couldn't really imagine that anything could be seriously wrong — not on a ship the size of the *Titanic*. After all, the weather had been calm and clear. "I lay quietly in my berth with my little girl and almost fell asleep again," she said. "In what seemed a very few moments my husband returned. He was a bit excited then.

A photo of the iceberg that purportedly sank the *Titanic*.

"'What do you think,' he exclaimed. 'We have struck an iceberg, a big one, but there is no danger an officer just told me so.'"

It wasn't long before Charlotte and Harvey began to hear the sounds of footsteps in the passageway. The noise reminded the young mother of rats scurrying.

Harvey said, "'We had better go on deck and see what's wrong.'"

>»·«<

While passengers like Lawrence Beesley first noticed something was wrong when the engines stopped, Daniel Buckley, a third class passenger in the bow of the ship (possibly on F Deck or G Deck), woke up after the collision to find water seeping into his cabin. "I heard some terrible noise and I jumped out on the floor, and the first thing I knew my feet were getting wet; the water was just coming in slightly."

Not long after, Daniel heard two sailors come along, shouting for people to get on deck. Daniel did so, but tried to return to his cabin for his life belt. He couldn't get back — seawater was now blocking his way. ". . . just as I was going down the last flight of stairs the water was up four steps, and dashing up."

>»·«<

Earlier, Colonel Archibald Gracie had said good night to his friend James Clinch Smith and headed off to bed, tired out by his morning workout. The impact startled him awake.

"I was enjoying a good night's rest when I was aroused by a sudden shock and noise forward on the starboard side, which I at once concluded was caused by a collision, with some other ship perhaps."

Jumping up, Colonel Gracie turned on his light and opened the door of his cabin. ". . . there was no commotion whatever; but immediately following the collision came a great noise of escaping steam. I listened intently but could hear no machinery. There was no mistaking that something wrong had happened, because of the ship stopping and the blowing off of steam."

Gracie could not go back to sleep. He rose, dressed, and went up to the Boat Deck. But as he looked around, Gracie was puzzled. He still couldn't see any signs of what had happened. In fact, there were no other boats in sight. He couldn't see any icebergs either.

It was all very puzzling. "It was a beautiful night, cloudless, and the stars shining brightly," he recalled. "The atmosphere was quite cold, but no ice or iceberg was in sight. If another ship had struck us there was no trace of it . . ."

Colonel Gracie decided to look for an officer, but none was to be found. After a while he came upon some fellow first class passengers, including James Clinch Smith, who told him that the ship had struck an iceberg and even made a joke about it. "He opened his hand and showed me some ice, flat like my watch, coolly suggesting that I might want to take it home for a souvenir."

The two friends tried to put the pieces of the puzzle together. Where had the ice come from, and what did it mean? One person had apparently spotted the iceberg itself; someone else passed on a rumor that the mail room was flooded and clerks were trying to transfer two hundred bags of mail to an upper deck.

All at once Gracie noticed something odd. It seemed to him that the boat had begun to list, or lean, to one side. Maybe something was wrong after all.

⋙•⋘

Like Lawrence Beesley, seventeen-year-old Jack Thayer only became worried when he realized that the engines had stopped. "The sudden quiet was startling and disturbing."

Jack began to hear muffled voices and running feet outside his cabin door. Curious, Jack threw on his overcoat and stuffed his feet into slippers. He called to his parents in the next cabin that he was "going up on deck to see the fun."

His father said he would get dressed and join him. Soon the two were walking on deck trying to find out what had happened. Shortly after midnight, the cold drove Jack and his dad inside. "There were quite a few people standing around questioning each other in a dazed kind of way. No one seemed to know what next to do."

⋙•⋘

Through the words of a saloon steward named James Johnson we know about one of the most important conversations that night — though what was said no one will ever know. Sometime just after midnight Johnson saw ship designer Thomas Andrews go down to the engine room, "and then I saw the captain directly following him."

We can imagine Captain Smith and Thomas Andrews

putting their heads together with chief engineer Joseph Bell. Andrews had been involved with building the ship from the beginning. Bell, the father of four, had been a chief engineer for twenty years, and had recently served on the *Olympic*. These men understood the ship better than anyone.

The evidence of severe damage was overwhelming: Within ten minutes after the collision, water was eight feet deep in Boiler Room 6. There was seven feet of water in Hold 1, and the mail room had in fact flooded. Pokes and stabs from the iceberg had caused damage in the forepeak (the most forward section of the hold located in the angle of the bow) and in five other compartments along the bottom of the ship known as holds one, two, and three; Boiler Room 6; and just aft of it, Boiler Room 5.

The damage was spread out across a wide area — three hundred feet, only about ten feet from the keel. The watertight doors, which were supposed to make the ship "practically unsinkable," would not be able to save her. With the exception of Boiler Room 5, the water had risen about fourteen feet above the keel in the first six compartments within the first ten minutes after the collision.

And so it was that around midnight of April 15, the *Titanic*'s designer knew two things that must have made his blood run cold.

First, this important, expensive, incredibly beautiful ship — a ship he and so many others had labored on for years — would sink in a matter of hours.

Second, there were not nearly enough lifeboats to save the 2,208 people on board.

⟫•⟪

Captain E. J. Smith returned to the bridge of his brand-new ship. He gave orders for the lifeboats to be readied.

Fourth Officer Boxhall had a question for him: "'Is it really serious?'"

"'Mr. Andrews tells me he gives her from an hour to an hour and a half'" came the reply.

If Andrews was correct, the crew would have only sixty to ninety minutes to uncover, load, and launch the lifeboats — lifeboats that had room for only 1,178 at the most.

The *Titanic* needed help.

Although this is the Wheelhouse from the *Titanic*'s sister ship, the *Olympic*, the two were nearly identical.

➤ THE *TITANIC*'S WATERTIGHT DOORS ◄

The *Titanic* was supposed to be practically unsink-able because she was designed with special features to protect the ship from leaks. The bottom of the ship was broken into sixteen main compartments, sepa-rated by walls or partitions called "bulkheads." These bulkheads had special watertight doors. In an emer-gency, the doors could be lowered from the bridge to seal off each area and prevent water from spreading into other areas of the ship. And that's exactly what First Officer Murdoch did as the *Titanic* approached the iceberg.

So why didn't the *Titanic*'s watertight doors keep the ship from sinking?

First, the damage from the iceberg was simply too spread out. The *Titanic* would probably have stayed afloat with any two of her most forward five bulkhead compartments flooded. It could even have floated if three of the first five leaked. (See the British Wreck Commissioner's final report on the flooding on page 246.) But the iceberg caused leaks in the first six com-partments along the starboard side.

Researcher David G. Brown and others note that the initial flooding of the first three holds and Boiler Rooms 6 and 5 came in through the bottom of the ship, not over the tops of the bulkheads. These pri-mary areas filled up from below, as did Boiler Room 4.

However, eventually secondary flooding occurred, as water poured down over the tops of the bulkheads once the ship's bow began to sink.

The watertight doors helped seal off the compartments from one another, but the tops of the partitions themselves were not sealed off. The bulkheads only went up vertically as high as E Deck. So, as the bow of the ship began to sink, water did begin to overflow the *tops* of the bulkheads, causing enormous stress on the hull. "The downward tipping of the bow created tremendous strain or stress within the hull because the stern was lifted out of the water," notes Brown.

In other words, as the first compartments filled from below, the weight of the water pulled the ship down. The bow sank lower. Later, water spilled over the top of the bulkheads and down into the compartments behind them. Because there was no way to seal off the top of each separate area, the water brought the ship lower minute by minute. There was no way for the ship to recover.

Titanic researcher David G. Brown argues that the ship might have had a chance to stay afloat longer by using her pumps — if Captain Smith had not ordered the engines to start again, causing Boiler Room 6 to flood even more.

Brown puts it this way: "Ironically, *Titanic* sank because water poured down from above, not up through the bottom."

e Russian East Asiatic S.S. Co.   Radio-Telegram.

S.S. "Birma".

Origin.Station.	Time handed in.	Via.	Remarks.
Titanic	11 H.45M.April 14/15 1912.		Distress ca Ligs Loud.

Cgd - Sos. from M. G. Y.

We have struck iceberg sinking fast come to our assis
tance.

Position Lat. 41.46 n. Lon. 50.14. w.

M.G.Y.

"Captain Smith . . . appeared nervous. He came down on
deck, chewing a toothpick. 'Let everyone,' he said, 'put
on a lifebelt. It is more prudent.'"
— Pierre Maréchal, first class passenger

A distress telegram from the *Titanic*, which was sent by wireless operator Jack Phillips
to the Russian Steamer SS *Birma*, shortly before the *Titanic* sank.

CHAPTER SIX
IN THE RADIO ROOM: "IT'S A CQD OM."

Joseph Boxhall hadn't stopped since the collision. Captain Smith had sent him here and there — to do a brief inspection, to find the ship's carpenter, to fetch other officers who were off duty for an "all hands on deck."

Before the captain left the bridge to talk to the chief engineer, he'd given Boxhall yet another job: to update the ship's position and bring it to the Marconi room so the radio operators could let other ships know where they were.

Using his estimate of the ship's speed, as well as her course and observations of the stars, Boxhall jotted down the coordinates as best as he could figure them — lat 41°46′ N, long 50°14′ W.

In 1985, the *Titanic* wreck was discovered about thirteen miles south and east of Joseph Boxhall's coordinates. The wreck's position is lat 41°43′ N, long 49°56′ W. Even with the ship drifting perhaps two miles before sinking, it's clear that the reckoning that night was somewhat off.

Boxhall grabbed the slip of paper with the coordinates, probably showed it to Chief Officer Wilde, and then took it to Phillips and Bride in the radio room.

There were no more jokes about SOS now. Jack Phillips was working the Marconi apparatus frantically, repeating the CQD again and again. But the very notion that the *Titanic* was sinking on her fifth night at sea must have seemed unbelievable to anyone on the other end of these messages. After all, just hours before, ships had been congratulating the *Titanic* on her maiden voyage.

In one exchange later that night, the *Titanic*'s sister ship, the *Olympic*, wanted to know if Captain Smith was steering southerly to meet up with them. But the *Olympic* was five hundred miles away. Phillips radioed back a terse message: "We are putting the women and children off in boats."

But there was one young operator who did get it.

Twenty-one-year-old Harold Cottam was the only Marconi wireless operator working on the *Carpathia*. This ship, operated by the Cunard Line, was a ten-year veteran of the seas. She wasn't built for luxury or to attract the rich. In fact, the *Carpathia* could hold only 100 first class passengers and 200 in second class. Most of the room was in steerage or third class, where 2,250 passengers could be accommodated.

Although Arthur Henry Rostron had served as the *Carpathia*'s captain for only a few months, he was an experienced seaman — competent, conscientious, and energetic. His nickname was "the Electric Spark." The *Carpathia* had left New York on Thursday, April 11, a day after the *Titanic*'s departure from Southampton. Carrying 743 passengers, she was headed for England and then Italy.

Since he had no one to relieve him, Marconi operator Harold Cottam had already put in two long days of work. A few minutes later and he would have turned in.

"It was only a streak of luck that I got the message at all," Cottam later told the *New York Times*, "for on the previous night I had been up until 2:30 o'clock in the morning . . . and I had planned to get to bed early that night."

Harold Cottam had put on his coat, and was ready to leave the radio room, when he noticed messages being relayed to the *Titanic* from another long-distance relay station on Cape Cod. He decided to contact the *Titanic* to make sure the radio operators were aware of these messages.

Cottam was shocked at what Phillips radioed back: "Come at once. We have struck a berg. It's a CQD OM. Position 41.46 N. 50.24 W."

Harold Cottam replied, "'Shall I go to the Captain and tell him to turn back at once?'"

The answer came instantly. "'Yes. Yes.'"

Cottam radioed that he would inform the *Carpathia*'s captain. Immediately he set off to find Captain Arthur Rostron, who'd just gone to his cabin for the night. When he got the word, Rostron didn't hesitate: The *Carpathia* would go to the rescue.

93

Usually the *Carpathia*'s maximum speed was about fourteen knots. Captain Rostron would do his best to beat that. He said, "I immediately sent down to the Chief Engineer and told him to get all the firemen out and do everything possible."

But Captain Rostron was taking a chance. His ship would face the same danger as the *Titanic* — ice.

≫•≪

Back on the *Titanic*, as soon as word came that the *Carpathia* was on the way, Harold Bride went to find Captain Smith, who then returned with Bride to the radio room to check on the *Carpathia*'s position.

Maybe, just maybe, the *Carpathia* could get there in enough time to save more people.

But when he worked out the *Carpathia*'s position, Captain Smith realized that the rescue ship was fifty-eight miles away.

Fifty-eight miles. That meant the *Carpathia* wouldn't arrive for about four hours.

We now know that the *Titanic* was about thirteen miles closer to the *Carpathia* than anyone realized at the time. In the end, though, that wouldn't matter — the *Carpathia* simply couldn't get there fast enough.

But the passengers on board the *Titanic* didn't realize that. In fact, many of them assumed that rescue ships would be there at any moment.

"To those who showed concern, a reassuring answer was forthcoming: 'There are plenty of lifeboats in the vicinity; they'll be with us any moment now.'"
— Violet Jessop

A life preserver that was worn by one of the survivors of the *Titanic*, Ms. Laura Mabel Francatelli.

A LIGHT IN THE DISTANCE

Stewardess Violet Jessop was dedicated to her passengers. She helped people into their bulky cork life belts and reminded them to put on warm coats, all without giving a thought to her own safety.

Most everyone seemed calm. And if people seemed worried, they were given a reassuring answer. Not only were there "plenty of boats" nearby, they would be there "any moment now."

⇒•⇐

First class passenger Emily Ryerson heard the same rumor about rescue boats. After being ordered to go to the Boat Deck wearing her life belt, her chief thought was "not to make a fuss and to do as we were told."

A little later, when she was ordered to go to the lifeboat without her husband, he told her to go along — he would stay back with his friend John Thayer (Jack's father). They'd be fine and would just take another boat.

Everyone believed, as Emily Ryerson said later, that there was "a circle of ships around waiting."

It is no wonder that passengers thought that rescue was close at hand. After all, some people could even see lights in the distance. Twenty-five-year-old third class passenger Olaus "Ole" Abelseth certainly noticed the lights of a ship not far away.

Ole had immigrated to South Dakota from Norway as a teen ten years before. He'd just been home visiting in Norway for the winter and was returning to America with his cousin and brother-in-law. Ole was a responsible young man. He'd volunteered to watch out for another immigrant, the teenage daughter of a neighbor in his hometown. And as the only one of the group who understood English, he knew his friends depended on him.

In fact, Ole had been trying to get answers to what was happening ever since his roommate had woken him shortly after the collision occurred. One officer had told him there wasn't any danger. But Ole wasn't satisfied with that, so he woke his traveling companions. They all put on overcoats and made their way up to the Poop Deck, the third class promenade area at the stern of the ship.

97

"We all went up on deck and stayed there. We walked over to the port side of the ship, and there were five of us standing, looking, and we thought we saw a light . . ." recalled Ole. "I said to my brother-in-law: 'I can see it plain, now. It must be a light.'

". . . it did not seem to be so very far. I thought I could see this mast light, the front mast light. That is what I thought I could see. A little while later there was one of the officers who came and said to be quiet, that there was a ship coming. That is all he said."

Ole decided it was time to go down and get life belts for everyone. That tantalizing light from the ship in the distance never came closer.

A little while earlier, Lawrence Beesley had been roused to leave his cabin again. This time by a shout from above: "All passengers on deck with lifebelts on."

He made his way to the starboard side of the Boat Deck. The noise of escaping steam made it hard to hear. He found that he was one of a crowd of people, standing around and watching the crew at work getting the lifeboats ready, arranging oars, and turning the cranks so the boats hung over the side of the *Titanic*'s deck.

"We stood there quietly looking on at the work of the crew," he said. It seemed pointless to offer to help, since the crew seemed to know what to do, turning the cranks so that the davits swung outward until the boats hung clear of the edge of the deck.

98

It was hard to believe there was any real danger. After all, Lawrence reflected, nothing seemed broken or out of place. It was a beautiful starry night. The ship "had come quietly to rest without any indication of disaster — no iceberg visible, no hole in the ship's side through which water was coming in . . . no sound of alarm."

All of that changed in an instant.

"Suddenly . . . a rocket leapt upwards to where the stars blinked and twinkled above us. Up it went, higher and higher, with a sea of faces upturned to watch it, and then an explosion that seemed to split the silent night in two, and a shower of stars sank slowly down and went out one by one."

A gasp went up from the crowd: " 'Rockets!' "

"Anybody knows what rockets at sea mean," Lawrence said.

There could be no doubt: "Everyone knew without being told that we were calling for help. . . ."

But the distress signals would only work if there were other ships nearby to see — and understand — that the *Titanic* was in mortal danger.

And that was not to be.

❊ THE *TITANIC* AND THE *CALIFORNIAN* ❊

Although the *Carpathia* would have had to travel for four hours to get to the *Titanic*, there was a closer ship: the *Californian*, a 6,223-ton liner, whose lights Ole Abelseth and others spotted — tantalizingly close but never coming closer — during the *Titanic*'s final hours.

The *Californian* had left Liverpool for Boston carrying cargo but no passengers on April 5. At about 6:30 p.m. on Sunday, April 14, her captain, Stanley Lord, who had been with the ship since 1911, sent a message to the *Antillian* warning of three large icebergs.

Captain Lord was extremely worried about the field ice ahead. On Sunday evening he doubled his lookouts and then ordered the *Californian* to stop completely because of the ice. Researchers now estimate that the *Californian* was between ten and twenty miles away from the *Titanic*.

Just before 11 p.m., Cyril Evans, the *Californian*'s wireless operator, sent a message to the *Titanic*, using the slang common among the Marconi operators: "Say, old man, we are stopped and surrounded by ice." ("Old man," often abbreviated as OM, was a common slang expression used by the operators to one another.)

But this message only made Jack Phillips, overworked by all the personal Marconigrams he still had to send, lose his patience at being interrupted. He replied, "Shut up! Shut up! I am busy. I am working Cape Race."

And, after all, Jack Phillips may have figured that by now this was old news: Hadn't the *Titanic* been getting ice warnings all day?

At 11:35 p.m., before Phillips began to radio distress signals, Evans did stop. In fact, he turned off the wireless apparatus and went to bed. But while several of the *Californian*'s crew, including Second Officer Herbert Stone, Third Officer Charles Groves, and apprentice James Gibson all spotted the *Titanic* in the distance, they didn't seem to recognize — or act correctly on — what they were seeing.

Both Stone and Gibson spotted the *Titanic*'s rockets, but Stone made the mistake of not presuming that these were distress signals — and acting decisively. At least one rocket was reported to Captain Lord, who was sleeping. He wondered if they were some sort of company, private signals. He instructed them to continue to try to make contact with the ship with a Morse lamp and let him know — yet he did not get up to check on the situation for himself or order the radio operator to be woken.

From the *Californian*, Gibson and Stone saw rockets from the unknown ship on the horizon, eight in all. They watched through binoculars as the *Titanic* disappeared, yet they seemed to think the stranger in the distance was steaming away. Nothing could have been further from the truth.

At 3:20 a.m. there was a new rocket — this time from the *Carpathia*. Captain Lord rose at 4:30 a.m. At 5:20 a.m., Cyril Evans was shaken awake and told to check the wireless, when he learned the truth about what had taken place that night. By 6:00 a.m. the *Californian* was on her way to the scene of the wreck. By then, there was nothing to be seen.

Would history have been changed if the men on the *Californian* had been more decisive? What might have happened if the *Californian* arrived on the scene after the first distress rocket was spotted?

Most researchers believe that while a few more lifeboats could have been lowered into the water for people to swim to, given the difficulties of rescue at sea and the frigid waters, even had she come in time, hundreds on board the *Titanic* would still have perished. But just possibly, more would have been saved.

No one can know for certain. What we do know is that everything seemed to go against the *Titanic* and her crew that night. The failure of the *Californian* to realize that a ship was sinking less than twenty miles away remains one more piece of the tragic story.

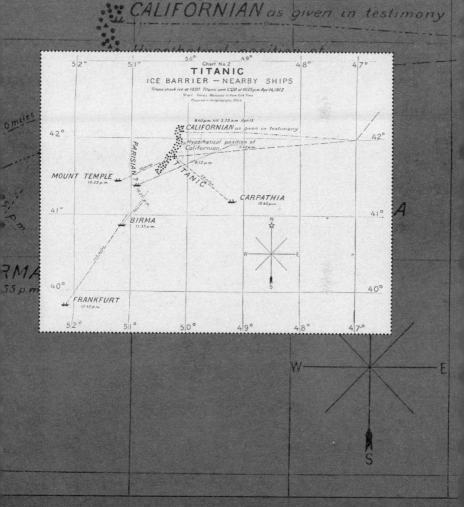

A chart showing the estimated positions of the *Titanic* and other nearby ships, based on testimony.

An illustration showing women and children being put onto a lifeboat from the B Deck.

"*Women and children first; men had to save themselves as they could. When Elna and I came up all the lifeboats were crowded, so no rescue was possible . . . You have to try to imagine it — the last moment I saw my dear sister stand there with little Thelma tightly in her arms.*"

— Ernst Persson, third class passenger

WOMEN AND
CHILDREN FIRST

12:40 a.m. In one short hour, the world had changed.

Instead of a triumphant arrival in New York City carrying hopeful families of many nationalities and the elite of society, the most magnificent ship in the world was headed to certain disaster. But most of the passengers and crew still didn't realize it.

While seawater continued to fill the compartments below and the boat now had a slight list to the port side, the flooding was not apparent to most. The changes were gradual, and not very visible. In other words, most people simply weren't aware that the situation was worsening from moment to moment.

※·※

Those on the upper decks could certainly see and hear the distress rockets Joseph Boxhall was launching into the moonless sky. Even so, there was no sense of panic. Most first and second class passengers had made their way to the Boat Deck or to warmer public areas on the upper decks, while many in third class were gathered on D Deck, waiting for instructions.

On the starboard side, First Officer William Murdoch and some crew members were getting the first lifeboat (Lifeboat 7) away, with Lifeboat 5 not far behind. Second Officer Charles Lightoller, who'd been off duty and asleep at the time of the accident, was now taking charge of the crew who were busy launching lifeboats on the port side. Launching the lifeboats took a lot of work; it took at least four men to handle the ropes as each boat was lowered from the deck to the water.

⇒⋅⇐

Below, seawater was making its way into and through the bowels of the ship. In Boiler Room 6, where the water had been eight feet deep just ten minutes after the *Titanic* struck the iceberg, the flooding continued unabated. The men had abandoned Boiler Room 6 as a lost cause.

While Boiler Room 5 was still secure, problems were beginning in Boiler Room 4. Sometime after 12:30 a.m., the crew noticed water seeping in over the floor plates from somewhere below. There had been no immediate sign of damage here, but by about 12:40 a.m. the water was approximately a foot deep. It's likely that the ship had been damaged on the bottom as well as the side.

Stoker Fred Barrett, who'd been in Boiler Room 6 at the time of the collision, had stayed below, helping the engineers working with the pumps and furnaces. Junior second engineer Herbert Harvey, age thirty-four and engaged to be married, had sent Barrett here and there on various errands as they worked to rig up pumps to keep Boiler Room 5 dry.

When another engineer, Jonathan Shepherd, tripped in an open manhole in Boiler Room 5 and broke his leg, Harvey and Barrett carried him to the pump room, a space at one end of the boiler room.

Harvey and Barrett kept on working. Suddenly, Fred Barrett saw seawater begin to rush in. Engineer Harvey yelled at Fred

106

to go. Barrett scrambled up an escape ladder as water surged in. He last saw Harvey turning back to try to reach Jonathan Shepherd. Both perished. Boiler Room 5 was now lost to the flooding. Fred Barrett made his way up to the Boat Deck. By now, a little after 12:40 a.m., he could see that the ship was tipping noticeably, "sloping down by the head." The mail room was filling and water was already within two feet of G Deck, and rising fast.

The first lifeboat was just being lowered to the water below.

⋙•⋘

Lifeboat 7, the first boat launched, carried less than thirty people, mostly first class men and women. (No one carried a stopwatch or was there to time the exact launch of every lifeboat. Most passengers didn't even know what lifeboat they were in. But by piecing together testimony from various crew members and passengers, we can arrive at approximate times. See the table of launch times on page 252.)

Lifeboat 5 followed three minutes later, with Third Officer Harold Pitman in charge. As Lifeboat 5 reached the water and pulled away, Quartermaster Alfred Olliver, also in the boat, noticed what most people were still not aware of from on board ship: The bow had already sunk fifteen or twenty feet.

Jack Thayer, wearing a warm mohair vest and an overcoat, tied on his bulky cork life belt and went to wait with his family in a noisy, crowded lounge on A Deck. His new friend, Milton Long, came by and asked if he could stay with them. There were no clear instructions of what to do. "It seemed we were always

This photo of the *Titanic*'s bridge and one of its lifeboats hanging from its davits over the side of the ship was taken by Father Browne. Captain Smith can be spotted looking down at the water.

waiting for orders and no orders ever came," said Jack later.

"It was now about 12:45 a.m. The noise was terrific," remembered Jack. "The deep vibrating roar of the exhaust steam blowing off through the safety valves was deafening, in addition to which they had commenced to send up rockets. Shortly

⇒ THE *TITANIC*'S LIFEBOATS ⇐

The *Titanic* had twenty lifeboats on the Boat Deck, but the boats were not all the same.

Fourteen were wooden lifeboats about thirty feet long that could carry sixty-five people each. There were two smaller wooden boats called "emergency cutters" with room for forty people. These sixteen boats were all known by numbers, with odd-numbered boats on the starboard side and even numbers on the port side.

The *Titanic* was also equipped with four additional boats with canvas along the sides that collapsed for easier storage. These four emergency boats (A and C on the starboard side and B and D on the port side) were made by the Engelhardt company and were often called the "Engelhardt collapsibles." Each could carry forty-seven people.

The upper decks of the *Titanic* were seventy feet above the water, so loading the boats meant swinging them out over the side and lowering them safely down to the water without tipping out the passengers.

we heard the stewards passing the word around: 'all women to the port side.'"

Jack said good-bye to his mother at the head of the stairs on A Deck, where she and her maid went out to board one of the lifeboats. The men decided to wander over to the starboard side. "People like ourselves were just standing around, out of the way. The stokers, dining room stewards, and some others of the crew were lined up, waiting for orders. The second and third class passengers were pouring up onto the deck from the stern, augmenting the already large crowd."

After a while, they made their way back to the port side to make sure Jack's mother had gotten into a lifeboat. Much to their surprise, she was still there. Now they were told that the lifeboats would be loaded from one deck below, A Deck. The ship was still only listing to port very slightly at this point. Jack and Milton Long followed a crowd, walking behind Jack's parents as they headed down to make sure that Mrs. Thayer could get into a lifeboat. Before Jack knew it, people had pushed between them, and he lost sight of his parents in the crowd.

"Long and I could not catch up, and were entirely separated from them," said Jack. "I never saw my Father again."

➤•◄

At about five minutes before 1 a.m. on the starboard side, governess Elizabeth Shutes was being loaded into Lifeboat 3, the third boat away. Right after the collision, an officer passing by her cabin had said that there was no danger. But when she'd stuck her head into the hallway a few minutes later, she'd heard the same officer say they'd only be able to keep the water out for a while. That's when Elizabeth knew the danger was real.

As she walked past the beautiful rooms of the ship, Elizabeth couldn't help thinking about the last few days: Here was where she had listened to a concert, this stairway had been full of happy, laughing men and women. No one was laughing now. As she passed stewards, Elizabeth noticed that their faces were as pale as the white life preservers they offered to passengers.

Then it was time. "Our lifeboat, with thirty-six in it, began lowering to the sea. This was done amid the greatest confusion. Rough seamen all giving different orders. No officer aboard," Elizabeth recalled. "As only one side of the ropes worked, the lifeboat at one time was in such a position that it seemed we must capsize in mid-air. At last the ropes worked together, and we drew nearer and nearer the black, oily water."

111

Like so many others, Elizabeth felt nervous about leaving the safety of the great ship. In that cold, black, moonless night her lifeboat seemed so small. "The first touch of our lifeboat on that black sea came to me as a last goodbye to life, and so we put off — a tiny boat on a great sea — rowed away from what had been a safe home for five days."

The people in the lifeboat didn't want to drift too far away.

"The first wish on the part of all was to stay near the *Titanic*," Elizabeth explained. "We all felt so much safer near the ship. Surely such a vessel could not sink. I thought the danger must be exaggerated, and we could all be taken aboard again."

But those in the lifeboats also had a view of the progress of the flooding that passengers and crew couldn't see. Sometime around one in the morning or a little after, lookout George Symons, from his seat in Lifeboat 1, noticed that seawater was washing over the ship's name at the bow (probably around D Deck). The water was continuing to rise.

⤜•⤛

Charlotte Collyer had an even harder time deciding to leave the *Titanic* than Elizabeth Shutes. Charlotte didn't want to go without her husband. She clung to Harvey's arm as she heard the orders: "'Women and children first!'"

"Someone was shouting these last few words over and over again. 'Women and children first! Women and children first!' They struck utter terror into my heart and now they will ring in my ears until the day I die," she said. "They meant my own safety but they also meant the greatest loss I have ever suffered — the life of my husband . . ."

Charlotte hung back, watching two other boats being loaded, holding on to her husband and daughter. The minutes kept ticking by, and still she refused to go. Then suddenly everything happened at once.

"The third boat was about half full when a sailor caught Marjorie in his arms and tore her away from me and threw her into the boat. She was not even given a chance to tell her father goodbye!

"'You too!' a man yelled close to my ear. 'You're a woman, take a seat in that boat or it will be too late.'

"The deck seemed to be slipping under my feet. It was leaning at a sharp angle for the ship was then sinking fast, bows down," remembered Charlotte. "I clung desperately to my

112

husband. . . . A man seized me by the arm then another threw both his arms about my waist and dragged me away by main strength.

"I heard my husband say, 'Go Lotty, for God's sake be brave and go! I'll get a seat in another boat.'

"The men who held me rushed me across the deck and hurled me bodily into the lifeboat. I landed on one shoulder and bruised it badly. Other women were crowding behind me, but I stumbled to my feet and saw over their heads my husband's back as he walked steadily down the deck and disappeared among the men. His face was turned away so that I never saw it again, but I know that he went unafraid to his death."

❖•❖

Charlotte Collyer was separated from her husband on the port side, where Second Officer Charles Lightoller was so strict about "women and children first" that his policy could well be called "women and children only." On the starboard side, First Officer William Murdoch, assisted by junior officers Harold Lowe and James Moody and other crew members, was more lenient. Male passengers were allowed into the lifeboats if no women could be found.

Luckily for him, teacher Lawrence Beesley ended up in the right place at the right time. Lawrence had been watching the crew when a rumor started that men were to get into boats on the port side. Almost all the male passengers in the group left, leaving the starboard side nearly deserted. Lawrence was never quite sure why he didn't go with the others. But the decision probably saved his life. A short time later, he heard a cry: "'Any more ladies?'"

Glancing down, he saw a lifeboat about to be lowered from the deck below. A crew member spotted him looking over the rail and called up, "'Any ladies on your deck?'"

When Lawrence replied no, the crew member told him he had better jump.

"I sat on the edge of the deck with my feet over, threw the dressing-gown (which I had carried on my arm all of the time) into the boat, dropped, and fell into the boat near the stern. . . ."

Lawrence landed in Lifeboat 13, with sixty-four people aboard. The lifeboat began to descend jerkily, foot by foot. The ropes and the gear creaked under the strain. Above, the sailors were trying to lower the boat safely. The crew in the boat kept calling up: "'Lower aft!' 'Lower stern!' and 'Lower together!'"

As Lifeboat 13 was being lowered, it was hit by a stream of water discharged from the Titanic's pump system. The water pushed the lifeboat astern, directly underneath the spot where Lifeboat 15 was coming down. Lawrence and the other people in Lifeboat 13 shouted up a warning, but no one on board could see what was happening.

Lawrence and one of the stokers in the lifeboat stood up and touched the bottom of the other lifeboat that was now swinging directly above their heads, trying to push their own boat away from it.

"It seemed now as if nothing could prevent her dropping on us, but at this moment another stoker sprang with his knife to the ropes that still held us and I heard him shout, 'One! Two!' as he cut them through," Lawrence said.

Just in time, Lifeboat 13 swung away, and the other lifeboat landed right where it had just been. Everyone breathed a sigh of relief. At last they were on the sea, with the mighty *Titanic* still towering over their tiny boat.

➼·➻

First class passenger Colonel Archibald Gracie was a man of action. He and his friend James Clinch Smith were not the type of men who were content to stand around waiting for instructions. Colonel Gracie escorted ladies to where they could board the lifeboats, although crew members weren't letting male passengers help load. He had to stay back to let the women through.

115

But Colonel Gracie kept busy. On his own, he asked a steward to help him find more blankets for the lifeboats. And later, as it became clear time was running out, he and Clinch Smith stepped in to help Lightoller and others load women and children into the boats.

Gracie described Lightoller at work: "One of his feet was planted in the lifeboat, and the other on the rail of Deck A, while we, through the wood frames of the lowered glass windows on this deck, passed women, children, and babies in rapid succession. . . ."

Colonel Gracie was on hand when Madeleine Astor, the eighteen-year-old wife of the American millionaire John Jacob Astor IV was handed into Lifeboat 4. Madeleine was pregnant, and her husband was worried about her.

Gracie described what Astor did next: "Leaning out over the rail he asked permission of Lightoller to enter the boat to protect his wife, which, in view of her delicate condition, seems to have been a reasonable request, but the officer, intent upon his duty, and obeying orders, and not knowing the millionaire from the rest of us, replied: 'No, sir, no men are allowed in these boats until women are loaded first.'

"Colonel Astor moved away . . . and I never saw him again," said Gracie.

❧❧

First class passenger Emily Ryerson and her three children were also waiting to get into Lifeboat 4 from A Deck.

"There was a rough sort of steps constructed to get up to the window," she remembered. "My boy, Jack, was with me. An officer at the window said, 'That boy can't go.'"

Emily Ryerson must have felt her heart pound in disbelief. Her husband stepped forward and said in a firm voice, "'Of course, that boy goes with his mother; he is only 13.'"

"So they let him pass," remembered Emily. "They also said, 'No more boys.' I turned and kissed my husband, and as we left he and the other men I knew — Mr. Thayer, Mr. Widener, and others — were all standing there together very quietly."

The water had kept on rising. After Emily Ryerson got into a lifeboat, she looked back up at the *Titanic*. It seemed to her that the Boat Deck was probably no more than twenty feet above the water.

❧❧

As more boats left, Archibald Gracie and his friend James Clinch Smith began to call out frantically, looking for more women. "'Are there any more women? Are there any more women?'"

Colonel Gracie could now feel that the *Titanic* was listing heavily to port. The deck was on a slant, and it felt, thought Archibald Gracie, as if the ship was about to topple over.

And then all the regular lifeboats on the port side were gone.

"'All passengers to the starboard side,'" Gracie heard Lightoller command.

It seemed to Colonel Gracie that "the final crisis had come."

⇉•⇇

For a long time, third class passenger Ole Abelseth and his companions had waited for instructions on the Poop Deck. Finally someone came and called for women to go up. Ole explained, "We stayed a little while longer, and then they said, 'Everybody.' I do not know who that was, but I think it was some of the officers that said it. . . ."

But to their surprise, most of the lifeboats were gone.

"We went up. We went over to the port side of the ship, and there were just one or two boats on the port side . . . We were standing there looking at them lowering this boat," said Ole.

"We could see them, some of the crew helping take the ladies in their arms and throwing them into the lifeboats. We saw them lower this boat, and there were no more boats on the port side. So we walked over to the starboard side of the ship, and just as we were standing there, one of the officers came up and he said just as he walked by, 'Are there any sailors here?'"

Ole was torn: Unlike his friends and relatives, he understood English. He had experience at sea. He could easily have spoken up. And it might be his only chance to live. What should he do? In the end, loyalty to his companions won out.

"I did not say anything . . ." Ole reflected. "I would have gone, but my brother-in-law and my cousin said, in the Norwegian language, as we were speaking Norwegian: 'Let us stay here together.'"

And so Ole and his relatives stayed in place. And as he stood in the confusion on deck, he happened to overhear an extraordinary conversation between two of his fellow passengers.

"Just a little ways from us I saw there was an old couple standing there on the deck, and I heard this man say to the lady, 'Go into the lifeboat and get saved.'

"He put his hand on her shoulder and I think he said: 'Please get into the lifeboat and get saved.'

"She replied: 'No; let me stay with you.'

"I could not say who it was," said Ole later, "but I saw that he was an old man."

⋙·⋘

Ole Abelseth's experience was typical of many third class passengers. Some made their way to the Boat Deck on their own. Others got as far as the main staircase on D Deck, where they were told to wait for further instructions. Some groups of women and children were escorted to the boats, but the men were kept back. Third class passengers did not know their way around the ship, and there was no clear path from the third class area to the Boat Deck. There were also gates separating the areas.

Twenty-one-year-old Daniel Buckley, on his way to New York from Ireland to try to make some money, described one man's efforts to get through a little gate at the top of the stairs leading to the first class deck. "There was one steerage passenger there, and he was getting up the steps, and just as he was going in a little gate a fellow came along and chucked him down; threw him down into the steerage place . . ."

The seaman had also apparently locked the gate, though it hadn't been locked before. Angered, the passenger who'd been thrown down broke the lock and went after the sailor. "He said if he could get hold of him he would throw him into the ocean."

Meanwhile, the lifeboats were being lowered — some not filled to capacity. Why not? At first many women didn't want to get in. Some crew members seemed to think that the boats would also be filled from decks below; others assumed that the lifeboats would stay nearby and wait for further instructions, or return for more people.

And, as researcher David G. Brown points out, people were simply not called to the boats in any clear way. The first women and children who went out into the cold night air were helped into boats immediately. But many more stayed inside, in public rooms, waiting for instructions.

There was no organized plan to fill the boats or make sure

third class passengers could find their way to the lifeboats. In fact, there were no organized plans at all.

❖•❖

Thirty-one-year-old steward John Hart was assigned to almost sixty third class passengers, mostly women and children, down on E Deck. Right after the collision he'd helped passengers into their bulky cork life belts, though some, he said, seemed reluctant to wear them and just wanted to stay in their cabins.

Many passengers did not really understand the danger. After all, Hart himself had begun by reassuring them that nothing was seriously wrong. The reason, he said, was "to keep them quiet." Language was also a barrier for a number of immigrant families.

For a while, everyone just waited for instructions. At about 12:30 a.m., the word had come down to Hart and other stewards to bring women and children up to the Boat Deck. It took Hart some time to organize a group. Hart testified that he escorted about thirty women and children to Lifeboat 8, but researchers question this as no third class passengers were rescued in this boat.

It would have been hard for these passengers to find the way on their own into parts of the ship where they had never been. As Walter Lord notes in *A Night to Remember*: "It was a long trip — up the broad stairs to the Third Class lounge on C deck . . . across the open well deck . . . by the Second Class library and into First Class quarters. Then down the long corridor by the surgeon's office, the private saloon for the maids and

120

valets of first class passengers, finally up the grand stairway to the Boat Deck." No wonder third class passengers needed a guide.

After escorting his first group to the boats, John Hart returned and organized about twenty-five people. He noticed two other stewards also leading groups of third class passengers to the boats.

But once again, the trip took time — time to gather a group of women and children together, time to separate them from men (Hart's orders were to not bring men), and time to get everyone moving along.

By the time Hart got to the Boat Deck with his second group of women and children, he could see only one regular lifeboat available on the starboard side.

"I took them to the only boat that was left then, boat No. 15," Hart told investigators.

As he helped the passengers in, First Officer Murdoch stared at him and asked, "'What are you?'

"I said, 'One of the crew. I have just brought these people up.'

"He said, 'Go ahead; get into the boat with them.'"

At 1:40 a.m., John Hart climbed into Lifeboat 15 (the boat that almost landed on top of Lawrence Beesley and others on its way down). Even if he had tried, he wouldn't have had time for another trip.

Although stewards like John Hart did their best, more third class passengers perished than in any other class. They were located farther away from the lifeboats. They were accustomed — by regulations and practice — to stay in their own areas and

121

wait for instructions. Also, unlike first and second class passengers, men in third class were not allowed to escort their wives to the boats, encourage them to get in, or see them safely off. For passengers who did not speak English, trying to understand what was happening was even harder.

Someone had opened the gate leading to the first class deck area for third class women at around 1:30 a.m. By 2 a.m., men were allowed up too. Third class passengers began to surge onto the upper decks.

But by two in the morning on the *Titanic*, it was already too late.

An illustration showing lifeboats being lowered along the side of the *Titanic* and into the freezing waters below.

"*Surely it is all a dream.*"
— Violet Jessop

THE LAST BOATS

A little after midnight, the *Titanic*'s designer, Thomas Andrews, had given the ship about an hour and a half to live. At two in the morning, she had survived past that estimate.

But time was running out. By 2 a.m., the seawater that had been pouring into the forward section of the ship since 11:40 p.m. had caused the bow of the ship to dip beneath the surface. This caused a slant to the deck, which was worsening minute by minute.

The decks in the forward part of the ship had gradually been filling, one after another: G, F, E, D, C. It's likely that the flooding had reached at least the bottom of the stairs on B Deck before 2 a.m. A Deck would soon be next — and then the Boat Deck. And it wouldn't take much longer.

Together the *Titanic*'s officers and crew members had launched lifeboats 8, 6, 16, 14, 12, 2, 10, and 4 on the port side, and 7, 5, 3, 1, 9, 11, 13, and 15 on the starboard side.

Four boats remained: Collapsibles A, B, C, and D. Collapsible C was stored so that it could be lowered from the davits where Lifeboat 1 had been, and Collapsible D, on the port side, could be attached to the davits Lifeboat 2 had used. But Collapsibles A and B were harder to reach. They were lashed right side up but out of the way, on the roof of the officers' quarters.

The chances of getting these boats down to the sloping deck, loaded with people, and safely away were dwindling with each passing minute.

Four small boats. More than 1,500 people still on board.

Twenty minutes to go. Two a.m. on the *Titanic* was the beginning of the end.

❖ ❖

Nine-year-old Frankie Goldsmith had woken up to find his mother rushing to get him dressed. His father told him they needed to put on life belts and get into a boat.

Far from being scared, Frankie was excited. The last few days had been an amazing adventure. He'd been able to climb on the rigging and catch glimpses of the *Titanic*'s heart, where men toiled nonstop, feeding the furnaces to keep the lights on and make the ship run.

And now here was another new experience — a chance to be lowered way, way down to the water in a lifeboat. Frankie was too young to realize that what was about to happen would change his life forever.

"We young kids had experienced such a good and exciting time the past several days all over the ship where young third-class lads had been permitted to go, that being allowed into one of those lifeboats, at last, was GREAT!

"'If we are going out in a lifeboat we'd better take something with us,'" he told his parents excitedly. So he stuffed his overcoat pockets with some of the fruit candies they'd brought along for seasickness.

From their third class cabin, Frankie and his parents made their way to the spot where a crewman stood by a gate leading up to the Boat Deck. Here was a surprise: Frankie learned that only women and children were being let through; his father would have to stay behind.

125

"Dad put his arm around mother, kissing her," said Frankie. "He then reached down, hugged my shoulders and said . . . 'So long, Frankie. I'll see you later.'"

Frankie didn't realize what that good-bye must have meant to his father. And like Jack Thayer, Frankie would never see his dad again.

Alfred Rush, who'd been traveling with them, was proud to have turned sixteen on Sunday. He felt grown up now. And perhaps that's why, although this crewman would have let him through with the women and children, Alfred jerked his arm out of the sailor's hand.

"'No! I'm staying here with the MEN!'" he cried.

Frankie's mother pleaded with him, but he would not go. Alfred Rush died in the sinking. His body was never found.

126

Frankie and his mother began to make their way as best they could to the lifeboats. It was not an easy route.

"Mother and I were then led with the other ladies and children to a steel ladder located just to the rear of the ship's fourth funnel. We all climbed it, and upon reaching the floor of the deck on the port side, the group moved forward, carefully, so as not to be tripped up by ropes and things lying on the deck, apparently left from previous launchings of the lifeboats."

As they approached the lifeboat, Frankie and his mother found themselves in a crowd of panicking passengers. Many from third class were just beginning to realize that almost all the lifeboats were gone. Men were blocking their way, crowding around Collapsible C.

Hearing shouts, a first class passenger named Hugh Woolner and a Swedish friend named Mauritz Björnström-Steffanson, whom he'd met on board, ran over and began helping the officers pull men out of the lifeboat to make room for women and children.

"I got hold of them by their feet and legs," Hugh said.

Caught up in the confusion, Emily Goldsmith wasn't going to let anything happen to her little boy. When a man pushed in front of them and blocked their way, she dropped Frankie's hand and pushed the man aside.

"Seconds later, we were helped aboard the almost-full lifeboat," said Frankie.

Frankie's mother, Emily, acted in the only way she knew to save her child. The two escaped in Collapsible C, the last lifeboat to actually be launched from davits on the starboard side.

As she watched Collapsible C being loaded, another mother, Emily Goldsmith's new friend, Rhoda Abbott, made a fateful decision. Rhoda and her two sons, Rossmore and Eugene, had also managed to make their way to the Boat Deck, climbing a steel ladder onto the stern and walking on the slanting deck over ropes still left from the boats already launched. But only women and children were being loaded. Since her boys were teenagers, she felt sure they would be considered too old and not let through. She didn't want to take that chance. Rhoda Abbot stepped back to be with her sons.

The boat was lowered without them. Then, all at once, J. Bruce Ismay, managing director of the White Star Line, jumped into it.

People would question Ismay's decision to save himself — when more than a thousand passengers, including boys like Alfred, Rossmore, and Eugene, would die — for the rest of his life.

⇒•⇐

After Jack Thayer lost his parents in the crowd, he and Milton Long wandered over to A Deck on the starboard side. They watched as the crew finished launching the lifeboats; Jack could make out some of the boats in the water beside the ship. They could hear the music of the band, which was still playing.

The two young men realized they needed to come up with a plan. "Long and I debated whether or not we should fight our way into one of the last two boats. We could almost see the ship slowly going down by the head. There was so much confusion, we did not think they would reach the water right side up, and decided not to attempt it," said Jack. "I do not know what I thought could happen but we had not given up hope."

So they continued to wait, sharing what they knew might be their last moments together. They gave each other messages to be delivered to the other's family.

"So many thoughts passed so quickly through my mind!" Jack said. "I thought of all the good times I had had, and of all the future pleasures I would never enjoy; of my father and mother; of my sisters and brother. I looked at myself as though from some far-off place . . ."

Still, Jack was young and strong. He figured that they would still have a chance if they could keep away from the crowd and any suction that might occur as the ship sank.

Looking back on these moments, Jack had one regret.

"I only wish I kept on looking for my Father," he said. "I should have realized that he would not have taken a boat, leaving me behind."

❧•❦

While the officers and crew focused on getting women and children into lifeboats, belowdecks the engine room crew was still hard at work, trying to keep the lights burning for as long as possible.

Lawrence Beesley remembered the bravery of those men, who knew they had no chance of reaching the surface, let alone getting into a lifeboat. ". . . to know all these things and yet to keep the engines going that the decks might be lighted to the last moment, required sublime courage."

129

Alfred White was one of the crew on duty in the main light room, or electric engine room, of the *Titanic*, located at the Tank Top level. While he knew the ship had struck something, he had no idea of the seriousness of the situation. Then, sometime after 1:40 a.m., he was sent up to get a report on how things were going. Getting that job was the luckiest moment of his life.

When he reached the Boat Deck, Alfred was shocked. "The sight I saw I can hardly realize it. The second funnel was under water and all the boats had left the ship," he said. It was too late to tell the others he had left below. "I could not get back as the boat was sinking fast. We did not know they were all at boat stations."

❧•❦

Second Officer Lightoller had been working so hard that he was sweating, though he wore only a sweater in the cold night air. With all the regular lifeboats away, Lightoller turned his attention to Collapsible D.

This boat had been stored under Lifeboat 2, which had been launched at 1:45 a.m. It was easy to pull up and lock the canvas sides and swing it out over the railing along the side of the ship.

By now, flooding had reached A Deck, and was beginning to make its way up the stairway under the Boat Deck. The Boat Deck itself was a scene of confusion. Panic had begun to set in among passengers who realized that almost all the boats were gone, the ship was sinking, and no help was in sight.

At first Lightoller could find no women, and he found his boat being rushed by men. So he had crew members form a chain around the boat and was eventually able to fill it. As people broke through, he fired a warning shot with his pistol.

May Futrelle was one of the women in first class who had hung back, not wanting to leave her novelist husband, Jacques. Even now, when it was clear that time was running short, she still hesitated. In the end it was her husband who realized the moment had come.

"'For God's sake go,' he fairly screamed at me as he tried to push me away and I could see how he suffered. 'It's your last chance, go.'"

May paid tribute to the men who stood back and urged the women and children to get into the lifeboats. They were magnificent, she said. "A few cowards tried to scramble into the boats but they were quickly thrown back by the others."

Her husband assured her he would get a place in another boat. His last words were, "'Hurry up. May, you're keeping the others waiting.' He lifted me into a lifeboat and kissed me goodbye."

The ship was being pulled lower into the sea each minute. Lightoller was standing partly in the boat to help May and others get in. At that moment he was given an unexpected chance to save himself.

"As we were ready for lowering the Chief (chief officer Wilde) came over to my side of the deck and, seeing me in the boat and no seaman available said, 'You go with her, Lightoller.'"

Lightoller refused and jumped back on board. He would take his chances with the rest.

Collapsible D was launched at 2:05 a.m.

Hugh Woolner and his friend Mauritz Björnström-Steffanson were on A Deck. They could see that the end was near. "Looking out we saw the sea pouring over the bows and through the captain's bridge," said Woolner. As the lifeboat came down from the deck above, Hugh cried, "'Let's make a jump for it! There is plenty of room in her bows!'"

His friend replied, "'Right you are!'"

So, as A Deck was flooding, the two men climbed over a railing and leaped into Collapsible D.

Hugh looked back to where they had been standing just seconds before. "The water was pouring in through the door we had just walked through. It rose so rapidly that if we had waited another minute we should have been pinned between the deck and its roof."

131

With both men safely inside Collapsible D, Hugh climbed over some women and children, got out two oars, and began to row away from the ship for dear life.

❧ ❧

Jack Phillips and Harold Bride were still at their posts in the radio room at two in the morning. Phillips had not stopped his frantic efforts to get help on the wireless.

"He was a brave man," remembered Harold Bride. "I learned to love him that night, and I suddenly felt for him a great reverence to see him standing there sticking to his work while everybody else was raging about. I will never live to forget the work of Phillips for the last awful fifteen minutes."

Harold Bride fetched his life belt from under his bunk. "Then I remembered how cold the water was. I remembered I had some boots, and I put those on, and an extra jacket and I put that on. I saw Phillips standing out there still sending away, giving the *Carpathia* details of just how we were doing."

Jack Phillips wouldn't even stop to put on his own life belt, so Harold Bride strapped it on for him.

Captain Smith came to the Marconi room. Bride recalled his words: "'Men you have done your full duty. You can do no more. Abandon your cabin. Now it's every man for himself.'"

It was time to leave.

❧ ❧

After launching Collapsible D, Lightoller turned his attention to Collapsible B, inconveniently lashed on top of the roof of the officers' quarters on the port side. Together with another seaman whose face he couldn't make out in the dark, Lightoller cut and threw off the lashings and got ready to throw the lifeboat down to the deck.

Lightoller heard the seaman call out, "'All ready, sir.'"

To his surprise, Lightoller realized that the voice belonged to Sam Hemming, who'd been helping him earlier. Surely Hemming had gotten into a lifeboat to help row long ago!

When he asked Sam Hemming about it, Lightoller received a cheerful reply: "'Oh, plenty of time yet, sir.'"

But there was not plenty of time.

Lightoller and Sam Hemming managed to get the boat unlashed and down from the roof. It landed on the deck upside down. Lightoller knew there wouldn't be time to launch it properly, but hoped that it might be possible to right it and hold it steady for people to climb into it before it floated away in the rising sea.

133

Lightoller began to move across the roof to the starboard side. Hemming had already left the roof, hurrying over to assist First Officer William Murdoch with Collapsible A.

Hemming spotted Captain Smith and heard what were probably the captain's last orders. "The captain was there and he sung out: 'Everyone over to the starboard side, to keep the ship up as long as possible.'

"He was by himself when I saw him last," said Hemming.

※>·<※

2:10 a.m. The *Titanic*'s bow was probably twenty to thirty feet below water by now. Cold, dark seawater was swirling around the forward part of A Deck, although the insides of the upper decks were still somewhat dry. The roll to port was increasing.

Pressure from the flooding was building in the interior of the ship. As one writer has put it: "The *Titanic* had a pressure fuse building inside her which was about to set off a catastrophic plunge forward, taking everyone by surprise."

And that's what happened.

"Just then the ship took a slight but definite plunge — probably a bulkhead went — and the sea came rolling up in a wave, over the steel-fronted bridge, along the deck below us, washing people back in a dreadful huddled mass," said Lightoller.

As the ship plunged forward, seawater surged over the Boat Deck. Many people standing near Collapsible A, including Rhoda Abbott and her two boys, were swept off the ship and into the ocean. Hundreds rushed toward the stern, which was still above water, to escape the surging sea.

Lightoller knew that trying to make for the stern would only postpone the inevitable dive into the ocean. He didn't want to get caught in a large crowd either. He was afraid that people would panic and pull him down as they lashed and grabbed out at anything within reach in a desperate struggle to survive.

From his perch on the roof of the officers' quarters, Lightoller saw a strange sight: The crow's nest, usually ninety feet above the sea, was now just above the waterline.

As the ship plunged, the cold, dark sea he had watched all night was now washing over his feet.

"I just walked into the water," said Lightoller.

A little earlier, after helping to load the lifeboats on the port side, Colonel Archibald Gracie and his friend James Clinch Smith had made their way to the starboard side. They too began to help with the last boats. While Lightoller and Hemming worked on Collapsible B, Colonel Gracie helped First Officer Murdoch and others get Collapsible A down from the roof of the officers' quarters.

Colonel Gracie couldn't help thinking, "What was one boat among so many eager to board her?"

A crew member shouted out, wanting to know if anyone had a knife to cut the lashings. Gracie tossed up his penknife. The men scurried to lean oars against the wall of the officers' quarters, hoping to break the fall of the boat so that this last hope would not shatter. Finally it tumbled down onto the deck, breaking several oars on the way.

That was the moment when the ship seemed to dive forward and seawater surged toward them. Colonel Gracie and Clinch Smith looked for the nearest high place. They tried to jump onto the roof of the officers' quarters. It was no good. Their bulky coats and clumsy life preservers got in the way.

As Gracie landed back on deck from his first jump, the water struck him on his right side. Thinking fast, he crouched down, and then, like riding a wave at the beach, he pushed off and leaped again. This time he let the force of the surging water propel him forward and up onto the roof.

He was now a little farther aft, lying on his stomach on top of the first class entrance above the grand stairway, not far from the base of the *Titanic*'s gigantic second funnel. Colonel

135

Gracie gasped for breath and looked around for his friend. But Clinch Smith — and many others — had disappeared from sight.

". . . the wave . . . had completely covered him, as well as all people on both sides of me," he said.

He had no time to grieve. The ship was now sinking — the deck disappearing fast. ". . . before I could get to my feet I was in a whirlpool of water, swirling round and round, as I still tried to cling to the railing as the ship plunged to the depths below.

"Down, down I went: it seemed a great distance."

❧·❦

Harold Bride was also caught in the wave.

136

Minutes before, he'd gone to where Lightoller and others were trying to free the last collapsible boats from the roof of the officers' quarters. "I went up to them and was just lending a hand when a large wave came awash of the deck.

"The big wave carried the boat off. I had hold of an oarlock, and I went off with it."

❧·❦

At about 2:15 a.m., just a short distance away from Colonel Archibald Gracie, Jack Thayer could see the water rising up over the deck, the ship going down at a fast rate, the sea coming right up to the bridge. The crowd kept pushing back toward the stern, which was still dry. Shock and terror showed on people's faces.

Without warning, the ship seemed to start forward and sink at a lower angle. Jack heard a rumbling roar and what seemed to be muffled explosions.

As the bow sank lower, the weight of the water was straining the ship's steel structure to the breaking point. Jack couldn't believe the sound: "It was like standing under a steel railway bridge while an express train passes overhead, mingled with the noise of a pressed steel factory and the wholesale breakage of china."

Jack and Milton decided to jump into the water at the last second and then swim as fast as they could away from the ship to avoid being dragged down by suction or hit with debris.

"We had no time to think now, only to act," said Jack. "We shook hands, wished each other luck. I said, 'Go ahead, I'll be right with you.'"

Milton went first, disappearing over the rail. Jack never saw him again.

Then it was his turn.

>>•<<

Ole Abelseth also saw that time was running out. ". . . we could see the water coming up, the bow of the ship was going down, and there was a kind of an explosion.

"We could hear the popping and cracking, and the deck raised up and got so steep that the people could not stand on their feet on the deck. So they fell down and slid on the deck into the water right on the ship. Then we hung onto a rope in one of the davits. We were pretty far back at the top deck."

Like Jack, Ole and his companions wanted to wait until the very end to leave the ship. By the time Ole was ready ". . . it was only about five feet down to the water when we jumped off. It was not much of a jump. Before that we could see the people were jumping over. There was water coming onto the deck, and they were jumping over, then out in the water.

"My brother-in-law took my hand just as we jumped off; and my cousin jumped at the same time. When we came into the water, I think it was from the suction — or anyway we went under, and I swallowed some water. I got a rope tangled around me, and I let loose of my brother-in-law's hand to get away from the rope."

One thought came into his mind: "I am a goner."

❧•❧

The ship was now in its final moments. As the bridge went under, the ship's funnels tilted forward. The weight of the enormous structures caused the cables holding the front funnel to snap. As it fell, the air filled with soot, and streams of sparks shot into the black, star-studded sky.

The gigantic funnel hit the sea with a horrific crash, crushing anyone in the water below it. It barely missed Collapsible B, which had shot forward from the port side into the water and was now on the ship's starboard side. The splash from the funnel hitting the sea tossed the lifeboat, throwing off some of those desperately clinging to it. At the same time, Collapsible A, which had originally been on the starboard side, floated to port.

These two boats, one now bobbing upside down in the frigid sea, were the last hope for anyone left on board or struggling in the water for life.

138

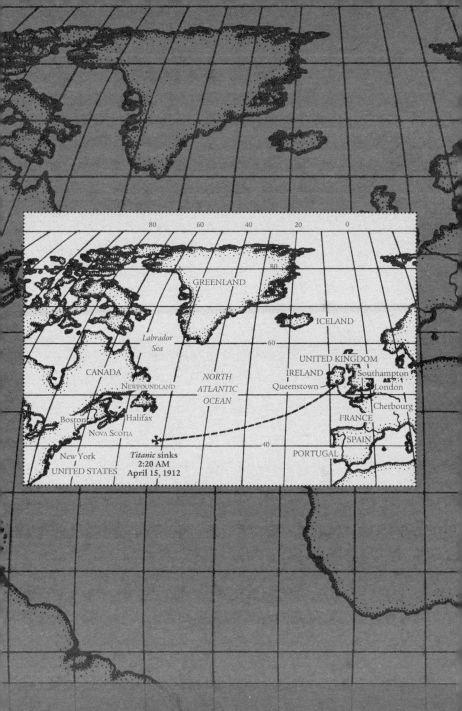

A map showing the *Titanic*'s ill-fated course.

"The water was intensely cold . . ."
— Charles Lightoller

An illustration that appeared in a London magazine, *The Sphere*, on April 15, 1912, shows the *Titanic* sinking as passengers in lifeboats watch in horror.

Some survivors watched the *Titanic* sink from lifeboats a mile away. Others, like young Jack Thayer, had a close-up view. *Really* close.

Jack was standing near the second funnel in the ship's final moments when his friend Milton Long slid down the side of the ship into the water. Seconds later, Jack threw off his overcoat and climbed onto the rail. But, unlike Milton, he jumped away from the ship, a decision that probably saved his life.

"The cold was terrific," he said. "The shock of the water took the breath out of my lungs. Down and down I went, spinning in all directions."

142

Shock? No wonder. The water was twenty-eight degrees Fahrenheit, below freezing. Painfully, deadly cold. Water that cold makes it hard to think or even to breathe. Fingers get stiff. It's almost impossible to grasp anything, to hold on. Most people begin to freeze in a matter of minutes.

Jack wanted to get as far from the *Titanic* as he could. He feared getting sucked down with the ship or crushed by falling debris. When he surfaced, lungs bursting, he was forty yards away from the foundering giant.

Then a strange thing happened. Jack knew — absolutely knew — that he should keep moving. He should find something to grab, look around for a lifeboat. His life depended on it.

Instead, he couldn't take his eyes off the unbelievable sight before him.

Jack saw hundreds of people on board rushing back toward the stern, which was now rising higher and higher into the air. The stern continued to tilt up until it was perhaps 250 feet out of the water. People trying to climb up toward the stern had a hard time. Many simply toppled into the sea as the angle became too great.

The noise was horrific. Everything inside the boat was crashing around — machinery, ovens, beds, mirrors, china, pianos, chairs, and tables. As the bow dropped below the surface, anything that floated rolled wildly in the water.

Anyone still inside the ship, especially anyone belowdecks, had virtually no chance of getting out.

All at once, Jack realized he was in danger from more than the freezing water. As the ship foundered, the gigantic second funnel appeared to lift off in a cloud of sparks.

143

"It looked as if it would fall on top of me," he said. "It missed me by only twenty or thirty feet. The suction of it drew me down and down, struggling and swimming, practically spent."

The ship was breaking apart. As the bow sank, the weight of the aft section, which contained the engine rooms, was simply too great a pressure for the hull to withstand — the hull began to fracture.

Incredibly, the ship's lights still blazed, thanks to the work of the engineers below who never had a chance at a lifeboat.

At 2:18 a.m. the lights went out, plunging the scene into an eerie darkness.

⟫•⟪

Minutes earlier, as seawater gushed over the deck, Second Officer Charles Lightoller had simply walked into the water. Like Jack, he was shocked by the intensity of the pain from the cold.

"Striking the water was like a thousand knives being driven into one's body, and, for a few moments, I completely lost grip of myself — and no wonder for I was perspiring freely, whilst the temperature of the water was 28 degrees, or four degrees below freezing."

Soon Lightoller found himself pinned against the wire grating of one of the *Titanic*'s huge air shafts — a shaft he knew went all the way down to the very bowels of the ship. He struggled and kicked for all he was worth, but it was impossible to free himself. ". . . as fast as I pushed myself off I was irresistibly dragged back, every instant expecting the wire to go and to find myself shot down into the bowels of the ship."

Lightoller realized he was drowning: ". . . another couple of minutes would have seen me through. I was still struggling and fighting when suddenly a terrible blast of hot air came up the shaft, and blew me right away from the air shaft and up to the surface."

Lightoller was in a precarious situation — caught in the chaos as the massive ship began to break apart. He got free of being pinned against the air shaft, but in the next instant he was sucked down against a grating.

And then, suddenly, he could breathe; he had come up to the surface again. By some miracle he found himself by Collapsible B — the very same Engelhardt emergency lifeboat he and Sam Hemming had wrangled off the roof.

Lightoller wasn't alone in the water. He could hear people

screaming around him. He had no strength to get into the boat. And even if he wanted to, he actually couldn't get in. No one could. The lifeboat had floated off the *Titanic*'s deck upside down — and it stayed that way.

Lightoller tried to catch his breath, hanging on to a small piece of rope attached to Collapsible B. That's where he was when the gigantic second funnel came crashing into the sea, barely missing him and the boat — and flinging them across the water.

He found himself clear, fifty yards away from the ship. "The piece of rope was still in my hand, with old friend Engelhardt upturned and attached to the other end, with several men by now standing on it."

Somehow, Lightoller found the strength to scramble up onto the bottom of the lifeboat.

145

⇒•⇐

One of those clinging to that lifeboat was wireless operator Harold Bride. He'd been standing on the Boat Deck near Collapsible B during the final moments. Somehow he had grabbed and managed to hold on to an oarlock when the water rushed over the deck, and as the wood-bottomed lifeboat was swept off, he was carried along with it.

"The next I knew I was in the boat, and the boat was upside down, and I was under it," said Harold. "And I remember realizing that I was wet through, and that whatever happened I must not breathe, for I was under water. I knew I had to fight for it, and I did. How I got out from under the boat I do not know, but I felt a breath of air at last.

"There were men all around me — hundreds of them. The sea was dotted with them . . ."

Harold Bride felt himself giving in to the cold when a hand reached down from the boat and pulled him aboard. "There was just room for me to roll on the edge," he recalled.

"I lay there, not caring what happened. Somebody sat on my legs. They were wedged in between slats and were being wrenched, I had not the heart left to ask the man to move. It was a terrible sight all around. . . ."

◈

After leaping from the ship, third class passenger Ole Abelseth felt the water close over his head. He didn't think he would ever come up. When he did, he found that another man struggling in the water had grabbed hold of his neck. Ole wrenched himself away and began to swim. He didn't see anyone he knew — his companions were gone.

He didn't know how long he had been swimming when he saw something dark ahead and made toward it. It was Collapsible A.

"When I got on this raft or collapsible boat, they did not try to push me off and they did not do anything for me to get on. All they said when I got on there was, 'Don't capsize the boat.' So I hung onto the raft for a little while before I got on.

"Some of them were trying to get up on their feet," remembered Ole. "They were sitting down or lying down on the raft. Some of them fell into the water again. Some of them were frozen; and there were two dead, that they threw overboard."

There was one woman on Collapsible A, the only woman to be plucked from the water into a lifeboat.

It was Rhoda Abbott. But she was alone. Her two boys had been torn from her arms in the sinking.

❖ ❖

Colonel Archibald Gracie had been swept off the roof of the first class entrance. He felt himself going down, right along with the *Titanic*. He swam underwater with all his strength. At first he worried that he might be scalded by hot water from the ship's boilers. But he needn't have worried; the killer that night was the cold.

Gracie knew he had to hold his breath longer than he ever had. "Just at the moment I thought that for lack of breath I would have to give in, I seemed to have been provided with a second wind, and it was then that the thought that this was my last moment came upon me . . . finally I noticed by the increase of light that I was drawing near to the surface."

147

Colonel Gracie was lucky. When he came to the surface he was near a wooden crate. He grabbed it eagerly. He thought that maybe he could find more debris and make a sort of raft.

All at once he heard a strange noise, a sort of huge gulp, from behind him. He turned his head to look for the ship.

"*I almost thought, as I saw her sink beneath the water, that I could see Jacques, standing where I had left him and waving at me.*"
— May Futrelle

Artists at the time of the disaster imagined the sinking in dramatic illustrations, not always accurate. Here, the *Titanic*'s stern rises into the air as the ship goes down; lifeboat passengers can only look on.

"SHE'S GONE."

"We could see her very plainly, badly down by the head," said Frankie Goldsmith. "All the lights seemed to be on when suddenly they all went out, and a loud explosion was heard."

Frankie and his mother had escaped in Collapsible C, one of the last lifeboats. Once on the water, Frankie's mother tried to keep him from looking back at the ship, forcing his head down so that he couldn't see. Then some of the ladies in the lifeboat cried out, "'Oh, it's going to float!'

"Mother then released me, and now beginning to be fearful about my father, I lifted myself to look past her shoulder and saw the tail end of our ship aimed straight up toward the stars in the sky," said Frankie.

"It seemed to stay that way for several minutes. Then another slight noise was heard, and it very slowly began to go lower . . ."

❖

Lawrence Beesley, safe in a lifeboat, struggled to describe the sounds of the dying ship. "It was partly a roar, partly a groan, partly a rattle, and partly a smash . . . it was a noise no one had ever heard before, and no one wishes to hear again: it was stupefying, stupendous, as it came to us along the water," he wrote.

"When the noise was over the *Titanic* was still upright like a column: we could see her now only as the stern and some 150 feet of her stood outlined against the star-specked sky, looming black in the darkness, and in this position she continued for some minutes . . ." he went on. "Then, first sinking back a little at the stern, I thought, she slid slowly forwards through the water . . ."

‹›‹›‹›

Charles Lightoller watched the final moments of the *Titanic* from his precarious perch on Collapsible B.

When the lights went out, ". . . the huge bulk was left in black darkness, but clearly silhouetted against the bright sky. Then, the next moment, the massive boilers left their beds and went thundering down with a hollow rumbling roar, through the bulkheads, carrying everything with them that stood in their way."

He knew the end was near. "The huge ship slowly but surely reared herself on end and brought rudder and propellers clear of the water till, at last she assumed an *absolute perpendicular position*. In this amazing attitude she remained for the space of half a minute. Then . . . she silently took her last tragic dive to seek a final resting place in the unfathomable depth of the cold gray Atlantic," he said.

Around him everyone breathed two words, " 'She's gone.' "

It was 2:20 a.m.

151

‹›‹›‹›

When Colonel Archibald Gracie turned around to look for the ship, he realized that the *Titanic* was nowhere to be found. The strange sound he had heard must have been the water closing over the stern in those last seconds.

Near him, three men floated facedown. A little farther away, he could hear the last, desperate cries of others who had tumbled into the sea.

Colonel Gracie knew he would soon lose his own battle. He threw his leg over the wooden crate to try to get his body out of the frigid water. It didn't work. He ended up doing a somersault under the surface.

A shape in the distance caught his eye. It was one of the collapsible boats, upside down, with what seemed to be a dozen or so men on top of her. It was far, but he didn't stop to think if he could make it or not. He set out.

When Gracie reached the boat, he grabbed the arm of a crew member and pulled himself up. He lay on the upturned bottom, gasping and shivering.

A tremendous sense of relief washed over him. "I now felt for the first time . . . that I had some chance of escape from the horrible fate of drowning in the icy waters of the middle Atlantic."

❧•❧

High-school student Jack Thayer had barely escaped being hit when the second funnel crashed into the sea. When he surfaced, Jack found himself near Collapsible B, and somehow managed to pull himself up and hold on for dear life.

Jack felt as though hours had passed since he'd left the ship, though he knew it was probably only about four minutes. From his perch on the bottom of the lifeboat he witnessed the ship's last moments, as the stern rose — and then sank down into the sea.

At first it was quiet. Then, there came a cry for help, and

then another. It soon became "one long continuous wailing chant, from the fifteen hundred in the water all around us . . . This terrible continuing cry lasted for twenty or thirty minutes, gradually dying away, as one after another could no longer withstand the cold and exposure. . . ."

Jack was struck with horror when he realized that no one was answering these cries. The lifeboats were not returning.

"The most heartrending part of the whole tragedy was the failure, right after the *Titanic* sank, of those boats which were only partially loaded, to pick up the poor souls in the water," said Jack. "There they were, only four or five hundred yards away, listening to the cries, and still they did not come back."

❖ ❖

153

Lawrence Beesley and his fellow survivors in Lifeboat 13 were shocked when they realized that so many people had been left behind to perish in the water.

"We were utterly surprised to hear this cry go up as the waves closed over the *Titanic*: we had heard no sound of any kind from her since we left her side . . . and we did not know how many boats she had or how many rafts," said Lawrence. ". . . we longed to return and rescue at least some of the drowning, but we knew it was impossible.

"The boat was filled to standing-room, and to return would mean the swamping of us all, and so the captain-stoker told his crew to row away from the cries," Lawrence later wrote. "We tried to sing to keep all from thinking of them; but there was no heart for singing in the boat at that time."

In Lifeboat 6, a group of women led by Margaret Brown (later known to history as the "Unsinkable Molly Brown") urged Quartermaster Robert Hichens to return to pick up people in the water. He refused, although later he denied it.

First class passenger Major Arthur Peuchen had been allowed into this lifeboat to help row, since he was an experienced yachtsman. He was disgusted with the quartermaster's behavior. ". . . we all thought we ought to go back to the boat. . . . But the quartermaster said, 'No, we are not going back to the boat. . . . It is our lives now, not theirs,' and he insisted upon our rowing farther away.

"He said it was no use going back there, there was only a lot of stiffs there . . . which was very unkind, and the women resented it very much."

154

❖•❖

In contrast to Hichens, Fifth Officer Harold Lowe had been busy organizing a rescue plan from the moment his lifeboat had touched the surface of the ocean. He began by transferring passengers from Lifeboat 14 into other lifeboats before going back with a near-empty boat to pick up survivors.

Joseph Scarrott recalled how Fifth Officer Lowe took charge of four other lifeboats, moving passengers to make room to rescue survivors from the water.

"Mr. Lowe decided to transfer the passengers that we had . . . and go in the direction of those cries and see if we could save anybody else. The boats were made fast and the passengers were transferred, and we went away and went among the wreckage," Scarrott later testified. "When we got to where the cries were we were amongst hundreds, I should say, of dead bodies floating in lifebelts."

Lowe had made an awful mistake: He had waited too long. It was probably after 3 a.m. when he began searching.

As the lifeboat moved through the water, Lowe and Scarrott could find only four people still alive. They pulled them all into the boat, but one, first class businessman William Hoyt, later died. The lifeboat remained mostly empty.

Another boat also picked up survivors that night. Lifeboat 4, with quartermaster Walter Perkis in charge, returned to the area where the ship had gone down and rescued eight people, although two of them died. This lifeboat carried Marian Thayer, Jack Thayer's mother; Madeleine Astor, wife of the millionaire John Jacob Astor IV; and Emily Ryerson and her three children, including her 13-year-old son, Jack, who had almost been turned away.

A bit earlier, as the ship was sinking, Lifeboat 4 had plucked someone else from the water: Sam Hemming, the seaman who'd been cheerfully helping Second Officer Lightoller to launch lifeboats almost to the last.

As the water was coming over the bridge, Sam had looked to see if he could spot any lifeboats. Off the starboard side, everything was black. But two hundred yards away on the port side he saw a boat. He slid down the side of the ship and struck out for it — without a life preserver.

When he reached it, Sam called out to Jack Foley, a fellow crew member he recognized. "'Give us a hand in, Jack.'

"He said, 'Is that you, Sam?' I said, 'Yes,' and him and the women and children pulled me in the boat."

155

Later, Sam Hemming was questioned by Senator William Smith, who seemed to have a hard time believing that the seaman had accomplished such an incredible feat. "Do you mean to tell me that you swam from the *Titanic* two or three hundred yards? . . . Two hundred yards without a life preserver on?" he inquired.

Sam Hemming assured him that he had. He had a life preserver in his room, but had never had time to go back for it.

Sam also told the senator that the water was cold. Very cold. "It made my feet and hands sore, sir."

Meanwhile, less than twenty miles away, the *Californian* slumbered on.

Later, crew members on the *Californian* reported that when they no longer saw the *Titanic*'s lights, they simply assumed that the unknown ship in the distance had sailed away.

Nothing could have been further from the truth.

Over the next minutes and hours, as a result of cold, exposure, and drowning, 1,496 men, women, and children would perish.

TESTIMONY OF HAROLD G. LOWE, FIFTH OFFICER
❧ UNITED STATES SENATE INQUIRY, DAY 5 ❧

Mr. Lowe: . . . I chased all of my passengers out of my boat and emptied her into four other boats that I had. I herded five boats all together.

Senator Smith: Yes; what were they?

Mr. Lowe: I was in No. 14. Then I had 10, I had 12, and I had another collapsible, and one other boat the number of which I do not know. I herded them together and roped them — made them all tie up — and of course I had to wait until the yells and shrieks had subsided — for the people to thin out — and then I deemed it safe for me to go amongst the wreckage.

So I transferred all my passengers — somewhere about 53 passengers — from my boat, and I equally distributed them between my other four boats. Then I asked for volunteers to go with me to the wreck. . . . Then I went off and I rowed off to the wreckage and around the wreckage and I picked up four people.

Senator Smith: Dead or alive?

Mr. Lowe: Four alive.

Senator Smith: Who were they?

Mr. Lowe: I do not know.

Senator Smith: Have you ever found out?

Mr. Lowe: I do not know who those three live persons were; they never came near me afterwards, either to say this, that, or the other. But one died, and that was a Mr. Hoyt of New York, and it took all the boat's crew to pull this gentleman into the boat, because he was an enormous man, and I suppose he had been soaked fairly well with water, and when we picked him up he was bleeding from the mouth and from the nose.

So we did get him on board and I propped him up at the stern of the boat, and we let go his collar, took his collar off, and loosened his shirt so as to give him every chance to breathe; but, unfortunately, he died. I suppose he was too far gone when we picked him up. But the other three survived. I then left the wreck. I went right around and, strange to say, I did not see a single female body, not one, around the wreckage.

> " . . . the boat we were in started to take in water. . . . We had to bail. I was standing in ice cold water up to the top of my boots all the time, rowing continuously for nearly five hours. . . ."
>
> — Marian Thayer (Jack Thayer's mother)

A photograph showing Collapsible B, which washed off the deck of the *Titanic* upside down. Seventeen-year-old Jack Thayer and others endured a tense night standing on the bottom of this boat.

A LONG, COLD NIGHT

At 3 a.m. in the North Atlantic it was dark and terribly lonely.

The moonless sky was peppered with brilliant stars. But the immense canopy above only reminded the shocked survivors of how small and vulnerable they were.

Their beautiful ship, a symbol of human achievement, workmanship, and technology, was gone. They were alone in their tiny boats on a great sea.

Twenty lifeboats drifted, one upside down.

A little more than 700 people were now in lifeboats; they were all that remained of the 2,208 passengers and crew. All the excitement and anticipation of the *Titanic*'s maiden voyage had turned to shock and sorrow.

Earlier that night, passengers had been enjoying dinner, music, and conversation. For some, an Atlantic crossing was familiar, but for many this had been the journey of a lifetime, a start to a new life in America. Now many families were ripped apart forever. Some people had lost not just loved ones, but their money and possessions. All they had were the clothes they wore.

As they shivered in the freezing air, the survivors could barely absorb the tragedy that had transformed their lives. Many were dressed lightly, unprepared for the cold. The lifeboats had few, if any, provisions — no lights, food, or even drinking water.

The disaster might have been easier to understand if there'd been a fierce storm, with pounding waves and howling winds.

But the night remained still and clear. The sea was calm. Dead calm.

Now, in the darkness of that terrible night, even those who feared they had lost their loved ones forever couldn't help wondering: Would help come in time to save their own lives?

⇒•⇐

From the time that Lifeboat 13 was launched, Lawrence Beesley realized that no one on board had the slightest idea what to do or where to go. If there was some sort of plan for the lifeboats, the crew members in his lifeboat certainly weren't aware of it.

"Shouting began from one end of the boat to the other as to what we should do, where we should go . . ." he recalled. "At last we asked, 'Who is in charge of this boat?' but there was no reply."

Finally everyone decided that it made sense for a crew member in the stern next to the tiller to be in charge. They also determined to try to stay as close to the other lifeboats as possible. It could be fatal to drift away.

"Our plan of action was simple: to keep all the boats together as far as possible and wait until we were picked up by other liners," said Lawrence.

Some people had heard a rumor that the *Olympic* was already on her way and would get there by two the next afternoon. Lawrence remembered one crew member saying, "'The sea will be covered with ships tomorrow afternoon: they will race up from all over the sea to find us.'"

But the *Olympic* was more than five hundred miles away.

⟫•⟪

Governess Elizabeth Shutes had been evacuated in Lifeboat 3, one of the first boats launched, at a point when it seemed impossible to believe that anything could happen to the great *Titanic*. In fact, she had been scared of leaving the safety of the ship.

Lifeboat 3 had no emergency supplies — no lanterns, biscuits, or fresh water. If help didn't arrive, or they drifted too far and got lost, they wouldn't survive long. Elizabeth didn't have much confidence in the crew members either.

"Our men knew nothing about the position of the stars, hardly how to pull together," Elizabeth recalled. "Two oars were soon overboard. The men's hands were too cold to hold on. We stopped while they beat their hands and arms, then started on again."

As the hours dragged on, Elizabeth felt her spirits sink further. "The life preservers helped to keep us warm, but the night was bitter cold, and it grew colder and colder, and just before dawn, the coldest, darkest hour of all, no help seemed possible."

She'd never seen so many stars. But the beautiful night just seemed to make things worse, to intensify the loneliness that everyone felt. All they could do was hope and wait for dawn.

⟫•⟪

In Lifeboat 14, Charlotte Collyer clutched her eight-year-old daughter, Marjorie, to her, and tried not to think about her husband's fate. That awful night was a blur.

"I have no idea of the passage of time. . . . Someone gave me a ship's blanket which seemed to protect me from the bitter cold and Marjorie had the cabin blanket that I had wrapped around her, but we were sitting with our feet in several inches of icy water."

The survivors were hungry and thirsty too. "The salt spray had made us terribly thirsty and there was no fresh water and certainly no food of any kind on the boat . . . The worst thing that happened to me was when I fell, half fainting against one of the men at the oars, my loose hair was caught in the row-locks and half of it was torn out by the roots."

But while these survivors were cold and in shock, they were relatively safe — so long as rescue arrived soon.

That wasn't true for the men on Collapsible B, the lifeboat that been swept into the sea upside down. Eventually twenty or more men found themselves perched precariously on its bottom, trying to stay awake, stay on, stay alive.

"We were standing, sitting, kneeling, lying, in all conceivable positions, in order to get a small hold on the half inch overlap of the boat's planking, which was the only means of keeping ourselves from sliding off the slippery surface into that icy water," recalled Jack Thayer. "I was kneeling. A man was kneeling on my legs with his hands on my shoulders, and in turn somebody was on him . . . we could not move.

"The assistant wireless man, Harold Bride, was lying across, in front of me with his legs in the water, and his feet jammed against the cork fender, which about two feet under water."

They didn't dare move, afraid of being thrown into the sea.

And it seemed to them all as if the air was leaking from under the boat, "lowering us further and further into the water."

"We prayed and sang hymns . . . Harold Bride helped greatly to keep our hopes up . . . He said time and time again, in answer to despairing doubters, 'The *Carpathia* is coming up as fast as she can. I gave her our position. There is no mistake. We should see her lights at about four or a little after.'"

Jack could only hope that Harold Bride was right.

❖·❖

Things weren't much better on Collapsible A, which, although right side up, had been swept off the ship before its canvas sides were pulled up.

Ole Abelseth felt lucky to be on it just the same. Though he kept swinging his arms to stay warm, it was a long, grueling night. "In this little boat the canvas was not raised up. We tried to raise the canvas up but we could not get it up. We stood all night in about 12 or 14 inches of water on this thing and our feet were in the water all the time."

❖·❖

As he balanced precariously with the others on the upturned bottom of Collapsible B, Second Officer Charles H. Lightoller began to think it would be a miracle if they survived until dawn.

The men were standing in their cold, wet clothes. They were in danger from hypothermia and exposure. Lightoller tried to do what he could to increase their chances and keep the boat from foundering. As the first faint streaks of dawn appeared, the only reason the men remained alive was that they had stayed huddled together.

In the early morning, the wind came up; the seas got rough. The waves lapped higher onto the top of the boat. The survivors shivered; the salt spray hurt their skin and eyes; their legs ached and their muscles strained to keep their balance. Their feet were freezing and numb.

At any moment, they could be thrown into the sea. To help keep the boat steady, Lightoller made everyone face one way, then another. He called out, "'Lean to the right,' 'Stand upright,' or 'Lean to the left.'"

Radio operator Harold Bride's feet screamed with pain. Unlike many others, he was lying down. He'd rolled onto the edge of the boat; someone was sitting on his legs. Icy salt water sprayed over his clothing. Toward morning, the waves were so high they covered his head, one after another. "I didn't care what happened," said Harold. "I just lay and gasped when I could and felt the pain in my feet."

Lightoller would never forget that cold and miserable night. "If ever human endurance was taxed to the limit, surely it was during those long hours of exposure in a temperature below freezing, standing motionless in our wet clothes," he said.

Charles Joughin, the *Titanic*'s baker, was also on Collapsible B. He did admit to having a tumbler of liquor after the collision. Whether that helped or not, he had incredible luck that night. He hung on to the outside rail of the *Titanic*'s Poop Deck until the moment the stern disappeared below the sea. He claimed to be in the water for over two hours, "just paddling and treading water."

"Just as it was breaking daylight I saw what I thought was some wreckage and I started to swim towards it slowly," the baker said. "When I got near enough, I found it was a collapsible . . . with an Officer and I should say about twenty or twenty-five men standing on the top of it."

There was no room for Joughin. "A cook that was on the collapsible recognized me, and held out his hand and held me — a chap named Maynard [Isaac Maynard]." Joughin somehow managed to hold on to the side and stay alive.

But not everyone did. No one knows exactly how many men climbed onto Collapsible B, or like Joughin, clung to the side. Harold Bride believed that senior Marconi operator Jack Phillips, who'd worked so hard to get help for the ship, hung on for a time before losing his battle with cold and fatigue.

Lightoller said later, "Some quietly lost consciousness, subsided into the water, and slipped overboard, there being nothing on the smooth flat bottom of the boat to hold them. No one was in a condition to help . . ."

At about four in the morning, the men on Collapsible B spotted a faint light in the distance. A ship at last! ". . . glory be to God, we saw the steamer *Carpathia* about four or five miles away, with other *Titanic* lifeboats rowing towards her," said Colonel Gracie.

But Lightoller wasn't sure the men on Collapsible B could wait until the steamer reached them.

They needed help now.

"*Even through my numbness I began to realize that
I was saved — that I would live.*"
— Jack Thayer

Survivors in a lifeboat make their way to the rescuing ship, the *Carpathia*.

RESCUE AT DAWN

Since the moment the distress signal arrived, the *Carpathia* had been steaming through the night toward the *Titanic*'s last known location. Captain Arthur Rostron wanted to go as fast as possible without endangering his own ship in an area he realized would be dangerous.

"Knowing that the *Titanic* had struck ice, of course I had to take extra care and every precaution to keep clear of anything that might look like ice," Captain Rostron later told investigators. ". . . I went full speed, all we could . . ."

Captain Rostron had no way of knowing how many survivors he might have to take on — or what condition they would be in. He gave orders for the cooks to prepare warm beverages: tea, coffee, and hot soup. The crew gathered all the extra blankets they could find. All of the public rooms, and the cabins belonging to the officers and to Captain Rostron himself, would be turned over to the survivors. Third class passengers were moved into closer quarters so that the *Titanic* survivors could have their berths.

⇒•⇐

The *Carpathia*'s wireless operator, Harold Cottam, had never gone to bed. He stayed in the radio room, monitoring messages from the stricken ship. The last one he was able to pick up came at 1:45 a.m., when Jack Phillips reported: "'Engine room full up to the boilers.'"

In the early morning hours, Captain Rostron guessed he

Captain Arthur Rostron of the *Carpathia*.

must be getting close to where the *Titanic* should be — though he had no idea what he might find when he got there. In the distance he spied one of the green flares Fourth Officer Joseph Boxhall had been sending off throughout the night from Lifeboat 2.

"Between 2:45 and 4 o'clock, the time I stopped my engines, we were passing icebergs on every side and making them ahead and having to alter our course several times to clear the bergs," reported Captain Rostron. "At 4 o'clock I stopped. At 4:10 I got the first boat alongside."

As the light broke, Captain Rostron and his crew scanned the waters. There was no sign of the *Titanic*. But they could see other lifeboats now, scattered over the area, with their loads of cold, shocked survivors.

⇒ JUST HOW CLOSE WAS THE *CARPATHIA*? ⇐

According to *Titanic* lore, the *Carpathia* covered fifty-eight miles in three hours and twenty-five minutes at an average speed of seventeen knots. With the discovery of the *Titanic* wreck in 1986 and further study of the *Carpathia*'s timing and course and the location of the lifeboats, we now know that was not the case. The *Carpathia*'s maximum speed was probably fourteen or fifteen knots. And the ship was probably thirteen miles closer than Rostron realized.

One by one, the lifeboats began to make their way to the *Carpathia*.

※ ⋅ ※

Meanwhile, as he struggled desperately to fight the cold and keep his balance, Jack Thayer could feel Collapsible B sinking lower beneath him. The pocket of air under the lifeboat was escaping faster. Icy seawater splashed higher against his legs with each wave.

Even as he looked at the steamship in the distance and its promise of survival, Jack felt his hope slipping away. "We had visions of sinking before the help so near at hand could reach us."

The men on Collapsible B could see the ship beginning to pluck survivors from other boats.

171

"The *Carpathia*, waiting for a little more light, was slowly coming up on the boats and was picking them up," said Jack. "With the dawn breaking, we could see them being hoisted from the water. For us, afraid we might overturn any minute, the suspense was terrible."

Then another welcome sight met their eyes. ". . . on our starboard side, much to our surprise . . . were four of the *Titanic*'s lifeboats strung together in line," said Colonel Gracie.

Lightoller had an officer's whistle in his pocket. He put it to his cold lips and blew a shrill blast.

"'Come over and take us off,'" Colonel Gracie heard him cry.

Gracie was relieved to hear the ready response: "'Aye, Aye, sir.'"

FROM THE ORDERS OF
CAPTAIN ARTHUR ROSTRON

TO PREPARE THE *CARPATHIA* TO
RECEIVE *TITANIC* SURVIVORS
REPORTED AT THE UNITED STATES SENATE INQUIRY

• English doctor, with assistants, to remain in first class dining room.

• Italian doctor, with assistants, to remain in second class dining room.

• Hungarian doctor, with assistants, to remain in third class dining room.

• Each doctor to have supplies of restoratives, stimulants, and everything to hand for immediate needs of probable wounded or sick.

• Purser, with assistant purser and chief steward, to receive the passengers, etc., at different gangways, controlling our own stewards in assisting Titanic passengers to the dining rooms, etc.; also to get Christian and surnames of all survivors as soon as possible to send by wireless.

• Inspector, steerage stewards, and master at arms to control our own steerage passengers and keep them out of the third class dining hall, and also to keep them out of the way and off the deck to prevent confusion.

• Have coffee, tea, soup, etc., in each saloon, blankets in saloons, at the gangways, and some for the boats.

• To see all rescued cared for and immediate wants attended to.

• My cabin and all officials' cabins to be given up. Smoke rooms, library, etc., dining rooms, would be utilized to accommodate the survivors.

• All spare berths in steerage to be utilized for *Titanic*'s passengers, and get all our own steerage passengers grouped together.

• Stewards to be placed in each alleyway to reassure our own passengers, should they inquire about noise in getting our boats out, etc., or the working of engines.

• To all I strictly enjoined the necessity for order, discipline and quietness and to avoid all confusion. Chief and first officers: All the hands to be called; get coffee, etc. Prepare and swing out all boats.

A chair sling at each gangway, for getting up sick or wounded. Boatswains' chairs. Pilot ladders and canvas ash bags to be at each gangway, the canvas ash bags for children to help get infants and children aboard. Cargo falls with both ends clear; bowlines in the ends, and bights secured along ship's sides, for boat ropes or to help the people up. Heaving lines distributed along the ship's side, and gaskets handy near gangways for lashing people in chairs, etc. Ordered company's rockets to be fired at 2:45 a.m. and every quarter of an hour after to reassure *Titanic*. As each official saw everything in readiness, he reported to me personally on the bridge that all my orders were carried out, enumerating the same, and that everything was in readiness.

Jack Thayer guessed it was about six-thirty in the morning when the other lifeboats drew toward them.

"It took them ages to cover the three or four hundred yards between us," he said. "As they approached, we could see that so few men were in them that some of the oars were being pulled by women."

One of the women in Lifeboat 4 was Jack's own mother. Jack was so cold and miserable, he didn't even see her.

⁂

When they made the precarious transfer into Lifeboats 4 and 12, Colonel Gracie helped Lightoller try to save one more life.

"Lightoller remained to the last, lifting a lifeless body into the boat beside me," Colonel Gracie recalled. "I worked over the body for some time, rubbing the temples and the wrists, but when I turned the neck it was perfectly stiff. Recognizing that rigor mortis had set in, I knew the man was dead . . . Our lifeboat was so crowded that I had to rest on this dead body until we reached the *Carpathia*, where he was taken aboard and buried."

Lightoller now took charge of Lifeboat 12, packed with about seventy-five men, women, and children. The danger was far from over.

Exhausted, cold, and in shock, the survivors in Lifeboat 12 had little idea of the peril they were in. The weight of the additional passengers from Collapsible B could sink the boat any minute.

"Sea and wind were rising," said Lightoller. "Every wave threatened to come over the bows of our overloaded lifeboat and swamp us."

$$\Rightarrow \cdot \Leftarrow$$

Elizabeth Shutes, in Lifeboat 3, had been keeping watch for lights throughout that almost endless night. She could hardly believe her eyes when the *Carpathia* appeared at last.

"All night long I had heard, 'A light!' Each time it proved to be one of our other lifeboats, someone lighting a piece of paper, anything they could find to burn . . . Then I looked and saw a ship. A ship bright with lights; strong and steady she waited, and we were to be saved . . .

"From the *Carpathia* a rope forming a tiny swing was lowered into our lifeboat, and one by one we were drawn into safety. . . . I bumped and bumped against the side of the ship until I felt like a bag of meal," Elizabeth remembered.

"My hands were so cold I could hardly hold onto the rope, and I was fearful of letting go . . . At last I found myself at an opening of some kind and there a kind doctor wrapped me in a warm rug and led me to the dining room, where warm stimulants were given us immediately and everything possible was done for us all.

"Lifeboats kept coming in, and heart-rending was the sight as widow after widow was brought aboard. Each hoped some lifeboat ahead of hers might have brought her husband safely to this waiting vessel . . ."

$$\Rightarrow \cdot \Leftarrow$$

A rope ladder is being fixed from a lifeboat to the *Carpathia* so survivors may disembark.

"It seemed to me an interminable time before we reached the *Carpathia*," said Colonel Gracie, now packed into Lifeboat 12 with Second Officer Lightoller in charge.

Lightoller felt the same way. But then, at long last, the *Carpathia* was only a hundred yards away. "Now to get her safely alongside! We couldn't last many minutes longer, and round the *Carpathia*'s bows was a scurry of wind and waves that looked like defeating my efforts after all. . . ."

Lightoller had been in a constant state of action since he had begun to uncover the lifeboats the night before. He must have been exhausted and cold. But somehow, through his skillful maneuvering, he was able to bring the overloaded lifeboat into the calm water by the *Carpathia*'s bow.

Bosun's chairs were lowered for those unable to climb up the rope ladder. Colonel Gracie, despite his ordeal, was able to move under his own steam.

177

"All along the side of the *Carpathia* were strung rope ladders. There were no persons about me needing my assistance, so I mounted the ladder, and, for the purpose of testing my strength, I ran up as fast as I could and experienced no difficulty or feeling of exhaustion," Gracie wrote later. "I entered the first hatchway I came to and felt like falling down on my knees and kissing the deck in gratitude for the preservation of my life."

Once on board, Colonel Gracie made his way to the dining salon, where he found that the women passengers on the *Carpathia* were eager to help the survivors get warm and dry.

"All my wet clothing, overcoat and shoes, were sent down to the bake-oven to be dried," he recalled. "Being thus in lack of clothing, I lay down on the lounge in the dining saloon corner to the right of the entrance under rugs and blankets, waiting for a complete outfit of dry clothing."

When he thought about all that had happened to him, Colonel Gracie was sure that keeping his cool had been the reason he was still alive. "I was all the time on the lookout for the next danger that was to be overcome. I kept my presence of mind and courage throughout it all. Had I lost either for one moment, I never could have escaped to tell the tale."

Gracie also knew how lucky he was — luckier than so many others, including his friend James Clinch Smith. Gracie could easily have been knocked senseless by debris during those chaotic minutes in the water. As it was, he'd taken more of a beating than he realized: He had a bump on his head, cuts on both legs, and bruises on his legs and knees. "I was sore to the

touch all over my body for several days."

Like Colonel Gracie, Jack Thayer was able to climb up the ladder onto the *Carpathia* on his own. "It was now about 7:30 a.m. We were the last boat to be gathered in. The only signs of ice were four small, very scattered bergs, 'way off in the distance.

"As I reached the top of the ladder, I suddenly saw my Mother. When she saw me, she thought, of course, that my Father must be with me. She was overjoyed to see me, but it was a terrible shock to hear that I had not seen Father since he had said good-bye to her."

Not long after, someone handed him a cup of brandy. "It was the first drink of an alcoholic beverage I had ever had. It warmed me as though I had put hot coals in my stomach, and did more too," said Jack.

"A man kindly loaned me his pajamas and his bunk, then my wet clothes were taken to be dried, and with the help of the brandy I went to sleep till almost noon," said Jack. "I got up feeling fit and well, just as though nothing bad had happened.

"After putting on my own clothes, which were entirely dry, I hurried out to look for Mother. We were then passing to the south of a solid ice field, which I was told was over twenty miles long and four miles wide."

A group of *Titanic* survivors on board the *Carpathia*, including Mr. and Mrs. G. A. Harder and Mrs. Charles M. Hayes.

179

For Jack, his mother, and the other survivors, the trip back to New York was "one big heartache and misery."

The only bright spots were the kindness of the crew and passengers on the *Carpathia*. Captain Rostron had given his own cabin to Jack's mother, as well as two other ladies: Mrs. George D. Widener and Mrs. John Jacob Astor, the young

Survivors of the *Titanic* rest on board the *Carpathia*.

widow of the millionaire. Jack slept on the floor for the next two nights.

"The passengers and crew of the *Carpathia* were wonderfully good to us, looking to our every need and comfort," he recalled. ". . . It seemed as if there were none but widows left, each one mourning the loss of her husband. It was a most pitiful sight.

"All were hoping beyond hope, even for weeks afterwards, that some ship, somehow, had picked up their loved one, and that he would be eventually among the saved."

Charlotte Collyer was one of these searching desperately for her husband.

"We could only rush frantically from group to group, searching the haggard faces, crying out names, and endless questions. No survivor knows better than I the bitter cruelty of disappointment and despair. I had a husband to search for, a husband whom in the greatness of my faith, I had believed would be found in one of the boats. He was not there."

Captain Rostron had found all the lifeboats. "By the time we had the first boat's people it was breaking day, and then I could see the remaining boats all around within an area of about 4 miles," he reported.

"I also saw icebergs all around me. There were about 20 icebergs that would be anywhere from about 150 to 200 feet high and numerous smaller bergs; also numerous what we call 'growlers.' You would not call them bergs. They were anywhere from 10 to 12 feet high and 10 to 15 feet long above the water . . . We got all the boats alongside and all the people up aboard by 8:30."

Captain Rostron arranged for a memorial service to be held, "a short prayer of thankfulness for those rescued and a short burial service for those who were lost.

"While they were holding the service, I was on the bridge, of course, and I maneuvered around the scene of the wreckage. We saw nothing except one body."

Captain Rostron had wanted to have one more look for survivors, just in case. Then the *Carpathia* set out to return to New York, the port she had started from.

The time was 8:50 a.m. on Monday, April 15, 1912. It had been nine hours and ten minutes since the most magnificent ship on the seas had struck the iceberg.

The *Carpathia* left the scene with the 712 *Titanic* survivors on board. There would be no more.

The ocean was empty.

183

≫⋅≪

Junior radio operator Harold Bride had suffered terribly from exposure and from having his feet crushed, frozen, and wrenched during the long hours on Collapsible B. When he finally reached the deck of the *Carpathia*, he could barely walk. He was helped below to a doctor's care.

But on Monday night, word came that the *Carpathia*'s radio operator, Harold Cottam, whom Bride knew, was overwhelmed by the number of messages he was being asked to transmit from survivors. Would Bride lend a hand?

Though he was still exhausted and in pain, Bride couldn't refuse. "After that I never was out of the wireless room," he recalled. He realized it was important for survivors to connect

A Marconi telegraph that was sent by a survivor of the *Titanic* from the SS *Carpathia*.

with family and friends. "I knew it soothed the hurt and felt like a tie to the world of friends and home . . ."

There were also inquiries and messages from reporters and newspapers. Bride ignored most of these. "Whenever I started to take such a message I thought of the poor people waiting for their messages to go — hoping for answers to them. I shut off the inquiries, and sent my personal messages."

It was, he thought, the right thing to do.

⟩•⟨

Titanic survivors gather on the deck of the *Carpathia*.

On the crowded *Carpathia*, survivors slowly warmed up and came back to life. And with that came the realization that many had lost everything. Several people formed a committee to take up a collection to help those in need.

Margaret Brown, also known as the "Unsinkable Molly Brown," who had spent the night rowing in Lifeboat 6, was active in these efforts. Once on shore, she also organized the

To be filled in when an Official Log is not delivered.

MARRIAGES, BIRTHS, DEATHS AND INJURIES

that have occurred on board during the voyage.

Date when married.	Christian and Surnames of both parties.	Age.	State whether Single, Widow or Widower.	Profession or Occupation.	Father's Christian and Surname.	Profession or Occupation of Father.

Date of Birth.	Christian Name (if any) of Child.	Sex.	Christian Name and Surname of Father.	Rank, Profession or Occupation of Father.	Christian Name and Surname of Mother.	Maiden Surname of Mother.	Nationality and last place of abode.		Signature of Father or Mother.	Signature of Master.
							Father.	Mother.		

FIRST CLASS PASSENGER DEPT

Date. 1912	Place.	Christian Name and Surname of deceased.	Sex and Age.	Rank, Profession or Occupation.	Nationality (Stating Birthplace).	Last place of Abode.	Cause of Death. See footnotes.
				Passengers Members of Crew			Supposed Drowning
April 15th	about	H. J. Allison	m			152 Abbey Rd West Hampstead London N.W.	
do.	41-16 Lat.	Mrs H. J. Allison	f				"
do.	50-14 Long	Miss Allison	f.				"
do.	do.	Mr Thomas Andrews	m	Ship Builder	Irish	Harland & Wolff Belfast	"
do.	do.	Mr Ramon Artaguveytia	m			26 Rue Pasquier Paris	"
do.	do.	Mr J. J. Astor	m		U.S.C.	Hotel Ritz Paris	"
do.	do.	Mr J. Baumann	m		U.S.C.	Grand Hotel	"
do.	do.	Mr Quigg Baxter	m		U.S.C.	Elysee Palace Hotel Paris	"
do.	do.	Mr T. Beattie	m		U.S.C.	Hotel Majestic Nice	"
		Mr Stephen Weart Blackwell	m		Passengers		"
		Mr J. Dorebank	m		Eng.		"
		Mr John B. Brady	m			Elysee Palace Hotel Paris	"
		Mr E. Brandeis	m				"
		Mr Arthur Jackson Brewe	m		U.S.C.		"
		Mr Archibald W. Butt	m	←	U.S.C.		"
		Mr Frank Carlson	m		U.S.C		"
		Mr F.M. Carran	m		U.S.C.		
		Mr J.P. Carran	m				

Under the heading "Cause of Death" should be entered, as fully as the space will allow, the chief circumstances attending the death.
If a fatal accident occurs at or about the time of any injury to the ship, or to any part of it, or to the cargo, the fact should be stated.
If a death occurs in port it should be stated whether it occurred on board or in hospital.
If a seaman dies on shore from an accident which happened or a disease which developed while he was a member of the crew, it is desirable that an entry of the death should be made in the same way.
As regards the account of wages and effects on form W. and E. 1 see note on the first page of this form.

Date.	Place.	Name.	Rating on board.	Nature of Injury.	Circumstances.
×	see No.118	Cairns Albert			

A list of drowned passengers who died when the RMS *Titanic* went down.

presentation of a silver cup to thank Captain Rostron.

Lawrence Beesley volunteered to help document the names of survivors and assist those who had lost all their money and possessions. "On the afternoon of Tuesday, I visited the steerage in company with a fellow-passenger, to take down the names of all who were saved.

"We grouped them into nationalities — English, Irish, and Swedish mostly — and learnt from them their names and homes, the amount of money they possessed, and whether they had friends in America . . . ," he said. "There were some pitiful cases of women with children and the husband lost; some with one or two children saved and the others lost. In one case, a whole family was missing, and only a friend left to tell of them."

187

Third class passenger Emily Goldsmith, who had lost her husband and all her possessions, didn't wait until they docked to begin helping others. Concerned about women and children who had only their nightclothes, she decided to take action. Frankie Goldsmith remembered that his mother approached the crew with a plan. ". . . she asked the men if they could round up any cloth or ship's blankets, scissors, needles, thread, and buttons so she and some of the other ladies could make emergency clothes."

While his mother worked, Frankie was befriended by Samuel Collins, a surviving fireman from the *Titanic*. He tried to keep Frankie's hopes up and took him "all over the ship — from up on the captain's bridge to down into the boiler rooms. I spent time with the cooks, the bakers, the engine room crew, all who tried lots of ways to cheer me up."

Frankie would never forget this experience. "Then it all came back to me — those wonderful sights we young boys aboard the *Titanic* had looked down upon, and that wonderful singing we listened to as the firemen were doing their job — and down here I was — *down there with 'em*!!!"

⤜•⤛

J. Bruce Ismay's behavior was in stark contrast to that of Frankie's mother and fireman Sam Collins, who reached out to help others as best they could. Ismay arrived on board the *Carpathia* in deep shock, asking only to be led to a quiet room. The *Carpathia*'s physician, Dr. Frank McGhee, gave Ismay his own cabin. Ismay made no effort to comfort the survivors or talk to families who had lost loved ones. Instead, he never left the doctor's cabin. Jack Thayer was asked to visit him, as he and his parents had previously met Ismay on the *Titanic*.

188

"I immediately went down and as there was no answer to my knock, I went right in. He was seated, in his pajamas, on his bunk, staring straight ahead, shaking all over like a leaf," said Jack. "I have never seen a man so completely wrecked. Nothing I could do or say brought any response.

"As I closed the door, he was still looking fixedly ahead."

A year later, J. Bruce Ismay retired from business. Charges that he had saved himself at the expense of other passengers who had not survived dogged him all his life.

⤜•⤛

Charles Herbert Lightoller soon realized that he was the senior surviving officer. Captain E. J. Smith, Chief Officer Henry Wilde, and First Officer William Murdoch had perished. Passengers eagerly turned to Lightoller with questions. Was there any hope that their loved ones had been saved by some other ship?

He felt he had to tell them the truth. "What kindness was there in holding out a hope, knowing full well there was not even the shadow of hope? Cold comfort, and possibly cruel, but I could see no help for it."

Stewardess Violet Jessop looked around for her friends and coworkers: "For our dear Tommy Andrews, for the good doctor, for the boys that made life aboard easier for us, for good friends in all departments. But they were all among the missing when the roll was called."

189

Violet was grateful to the *Carpathia*'s crew for their kindness. "But there was little that could be done to comfort those who had lost and knew it should not have been."

Lawrence Beesley was also thinking about the causes of the disaster. On Wednesday, after learning more about the ice warnings that had been sent to the *Titanic* before the collision, he sat down and wrote a letter to the editor of the *London Times* to tell the world what had happened.

He made a number of suggestions. Passenger ships crossing the Atlantic, he declared, should have enough space in their lifeboats for everyone on board.

And when they encounter a region of ice, wrote Beesley, ships should slow down.

Some of the *Titanic*'s lifeboats collected on the deck of the *Carpathia*.

Titanic crew members pose in their life jackets after their rescue from the sinking ship.

LAWRENCE BEESLEY'S LETTER TO THE *LONDON TIMES*

"Sir: As one of few surviving Englishmen from the Titanic, which sank in mid-Atlantic on Monday morning last, I am asking you to lay before your readers a few facts concerning the disaster, in the hope that something may be done in the near future to ensure the safety of that portion of the traveling public who use the Atlantic highway for business or pleasure. . . ."

He then summarized several points — the *Titanic* was in a region of icebergs, it was running at a high rate of speed, there were not enough lifeboats. He then made the following simple suggestions:

"First, that no vessel should be allowed to leave a British port without sufficient boat and other accommodation to allow each passenger and member of the crew a seat; and that at the time of booking this fact should be pointed out to a passenger, and the number of the seat in the particular boat allotted to him then.

"Second, that as soon as is practicable after sailing each passenger should go through boat drill in company with the crew assigned to his boat.

"Third, that each passenger boat engaged in the Transatlantic service should be instructed to slow down a few knots when in the iceberg region, and should be fitted with an efficient searchlight."

"The final docking in New York at Pier No. 54 North River, when all our friends and relations learned the truth about the extent of the loss, was the last nerve-shattering blow for many people . . . it marked the end of all hope."

— Jack Thayer

An anxious crowd gathers outside the London offices of the White Star Line, seeking news of the *Titanic*.

CHAPTER FOURTEEN
AFTERMATH:
THE END OF ALL HOPE

On Tuesday morning, April 16, the headline on the front page of the *New York Times* broke the first news of the tragedy: "Titanic Sinks Four Hours After Hitting Iceberg."

The *Times* had gotten hold of wireless telegraph reports of the *Titanic*'s distress signals on Monday night. A new age of immediate media coverage was ushered in; the reputation of the *New York Times* as a major national newspaper grew, thanks to its early breaking of the story and coverage of the event.

By the time the *Carpathia* docked in New York on Thursday evening, April 18, intense interest in the disaster had spread worldwide. Newspapers issued special editions. White Star offices were crowded with people eager for news. The flags of all ships in New York Harbor were flown at half mast.

As the *Carpathia* glided toward Pier 54, she was surrounded by tugs. Reporters shouted out questions. More than 30,000 people waited in the rain, huddled under black umbrellas. Police had strung ropes to allow the survivors to pass. The usual customs inspections didn't take place.

Souvenir hunters were already out in full force. On Thursday night, people stole oars and equipment from the *Titanic*'s lifeboats, which had been unloaded from the *Carpathia*. But interest in *Titanic* memorabilia had begun even earlier. James and Mabel Fenwick, a honeymoon couple on board the *Carpathia*,

196

discovered a hardtack biscuit in a *Titanic* lifeboat and kept it, passing it down as a family keepsake.

Colonel Archibald Gracie regretted not keeping his life belt. After moving from Collapsible B into Lifeboat 12, he huddled under a steamer rug with other passengers before reaching the rescue ship.

"My life-belt was wet and uncomfortable and I threw it overboard . . . I regret I did not preserve it as a relic," said Gracie.

Perhaps he should have. Genuine souvenirs of the *Titanic* have only increased in value over time. Christie's auction house has sold a brass name plate from one of the *Titanic*'s lifeboats for $60,000, while just a fragment from a life belt has fetched more than $11,000.

⇒•⇐

Survivor Lawrence Beesley was very glad to see land again. It seemed to him that eight weeks rather than eight days had passed since he'd left England. He could barely remember those first peaceful, uneventful hours of the voyage.

And, even then, he understood that his life would never be the same. "I think we all realized that time may be measured more by events than by seconds and minutes: what the astronomer would call 2:20 a.m. April 15, 1912, the survivors called 'the sinking of the *Titanic*,'" he said.

What Lawrence couldn't know was that a century later, even after all survivors had passed away, people around the world would still remember this date and time, and continue to commemorate the sinking of the *Titanic*.

"All the News That's Fit to Print."

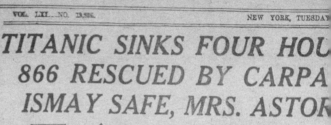

"All the News That's Fit to Print."

The New

VOL. LXI...NO. 19,806.

NEW YORK, TUESDAY

TITANIC SINKS FOUR HOU
866 RESCUED BY CARPA
ISMAY SAFE, MRS. ASTOR

Col. Astor and Bride, Isidor Straus and Wife, and Maj. Butt Aboard.

"RULE OF SEA" FOLLOWED

Women and Children Put Over In Lifeboats and Are Supposed to be Safe on Carpathia.

PICKED UP AFTER 8 HOURS

Vincent Astor Calls at White Star Office for News of His Father and Leaves Weeping.

FRANKLIN HOPEFUL ALL DAY

Manager of the Line Insisted Titanic Was Unsinkable Even After She Had Gone Down.

HEAD OF THE LINE ABOARD

J. Bruce Ismay Making First Trip on Gigantic Ship That Was to Surpass All Others.

The April 16, 1912, headline of the *New York Times* announces the sinking of the *Titanic*.

Crowds gather in New York City to read the bulletin board of the *New York American* to learn about the disaster of the *Titanic*.

A huge crowd forms outside the New York City offices of the White Star Line, awaiting news of the *Titanic*.

A newsboy sells the *Evening News* announcing the sinking of the *Titanic*.

❖

Harold Bride had played a key role in the *Titanic*'s efforts to get assistance from other ships. When the *Carpathia* arrived in New York, he found himself at the center of the media's interest. He sold his story to the *New York Times* and was happy to receive the money.

It would take Bride until the end of April to begin to feel better. By then he could say, "I am glad to say I can now walk around, the sprain in my left foot being much better, though my right foot remains numbed from the exposure and cold but causes me no pain [or] inconvenience whatever."

Harold Bride returned to England. He never forgot the dedication of Jack Phillips, who had continued at his post sending distress signals until the very end. Bride married and moved to Scotland. He and his wife had three children.

They named one of them Jack.

❖

Although she knew in her heart it was unlikely, stewardess Violet Jessop couldn't help holding out hope for a miracle: that another ship had somehow picked up survivors.

"In the dusk of evening, we crept up the Hudson into New York, where a crowd waited, hoping against hope that messages received had been false and that relatives might be among those on board," wrote Violet.

"Long before we got near the dock, despairing inquires were shouted across the intervening waters. It was only then that we learned that no other ship had found a soul. The horror was renewed all over again."

Wireless operator Harold Bride suffered badly injured feet in the *Titanic* disaster.

The next day, recalled Violet, some people brought used clothing they'd collected to the dock and spread the items out on tables for survivors. It reminded her of a rummage sale. Her thoughts were on getting back home, though it was hard to face another voyage at sea.

Brooklyn, New York
Sun April 21

My dear Mother and all,

I don't know how to write to you or what to say, I feel I shall go mad sometimes but dear as much as my heart aches it aches for you too for he is your son and the best that ever lived. I had not given up hope till today that he might be found but I'm told all boats are accounted for. Oh mother how can I live without him. I wish I'd gone with him if they had not wrenched Madge from me I should have stayed and gone with him. But they threw her into the boat and pulled me in too but he was so calm and I know he would rather I lived for her little sake otherwise she would have been an orphan. The agony of that night can never be told . . . I haven't a thing in the world that was his only his rings. Everything we had went down . . .

Charlotte Collyer

Violet Jessop went back to Great Britain on the *Lapland*, on a more southerly route than the *Titanic* had taken. Two weeks after the British inquiry into the *Titanic* disaster, Violet Jessop was on another ship — back on the job.

The *Titanic* was not the only maritime disaster Violet survived. During World War I, she served as a volunteer nurse for the British. Exhausted and sick after a tour of hospital duty, she was assigned to sea duty on board the *Britannic*, sister ship of the *Titanic*.

Violet was on board on November 21, 1916, when the hospital ship struck a mine off the Greek island of Kea and sank in fifty-five minutes, with the loss of thirty lives. Violet was nearly killed by the ship's propellers when she jumped into the sea from her lifeboat. She had never been underwater before and could not swim. Her life jacket came loose and couldn't support her. She managed to grab another life belt floating nearby. Before her eyes the ship took its final plunge.

Violet Jessop was pulled from the water by another lifeboat. She returned to work for the White Star Line in 1920, serving on the *Olympic*, where she had once been a stewardess before joining the *Titanic*. She continued at sea until she retired in 1950.

⋙ ⋘

Frankie Goldsmith and his mother, Emily, arrived in New York destitute. Although they only received fifteen dollars from the White Star Line and two railroad tickets to Detroit, other groups, including the *Titanic* Women's Relief Committee and the Red

Cross, provided financial assistance to them and other families in need.

Emily and her son kept in touch with several friends they'd met on the voyage, such as fireman Sam Collins and Rhoda Abbott, who had lost her two sons and was the only woman rescued from the water.

In a letter to Emily Goldsmith in early 1914, Rhoda Abbott wrote: "I read by the papers the terrible weather you are having. I suppose Frank enjoys it. I know my little fellow used to when he was alive. I have his sled now that he used to enjoy so much, bless his little heart. I know he is safe in God's keeping, but I miss him So Much."

As an adult, Frank Goldsmith continued to keep in touch with and search for other survivors of the disaster. He gave radio and television interviews on *Titanic* anniversaries, and was active in the *Titanic* Historical Society. When Frank passed away in 1982, his ashes were scattered in the North Atlantic, near the spot where his father had perished seventy years before.

209

❖

The United States Senate lost no time in calling for an investigation of the *Titanic* disaster. After all, some of the wealthiest men of business and most prominent members of society had perished.

In the days from the first inkling of the tragedy until the *Carpathia*'s arrival in New York City, newspapers, families, and politicians had many questions. But above all there was

The U.S. Senate Investigating Committee questions individuals about the *Titanic* disaster at the Waldorf-Astoria in New York City.

disbelief: How could the world's largest and safest vessel have sunk so quickly, with so much loss of life?

On Wednesday, April 17, 1912, Senator William Alden Smith proposed that an investigation be held under the Senate Commerce Committee. His Senate resolution called for a panel to be formed to "investigate the causes leading to the wreck of the White Star liner *Titanic*, with its attendant loss of life so shocking to the civilized world."

Senator Smith boarded the *Carpathia* as it was docking on Thursday evening, April 18. He spoke to J. Bruce Ismay personally, to ensure that he and employees of the White Star Line would cooperate with the hearings that, incredibly, were begun the very next morning, on Friday, April 19, at the Waldorf-Astoria hotel in New York City. The first witness called was J. Bruce Ismay himself.

The United States inquiry was followed by one in Great Britain, which lasted until July. In the end, the British investigation, sometimes called the Mersey Commission since it was led by Lord Mersey (Charles Bigham), did not find either Captain E. J. Smith or J. Bruce Ismay guilty of negligence.

But in its final report, the commission made a number of recommendations for the future, including twenty-four-hour-a-day wireless operators on duty, frequent lifeboat drills, and, most important, that there should be enough lifeboats and seats in them for every person on board.

❖

Colonel Archibald Gracie was an amateur historian. So it's not surprising that he began talking with other survivors right away, even while they were still on board the *Carpathia*, to document the events of the disaster.

He noted in his book, originally published in 1913 as *The Truth About the Titanic*, that he felt an obligation to write about what happened.

"As the sole survivor of all the men passengers of the *Titanic* stationed during the loading of six or more lifeboats with women and children on the port side of the ship, forward on the glass-sheltered Deck A, and later on the Boat Deck above, it is my duty to bear testimony to the heroism on the part of all concerned. First, to my men companions who calmly stood by until the lifeboats had departed loaded with women and the available complement of crew . . .

213

CONCLUSIONS OF THE BRITISH WRECK COMMISSIONER'S REPORT

The Court, having carefully inquired into the circumstances of the above mentioned shipping casualty, finds, for the reasons appearing in the annex hereto, that the loss of the said ship was due to collision with an iceberg, brought about by the excessive speed at which the ship was being navigated.

Dated this 30th day of July, 1912.
MERSEY.
Wreck Commissioner.

Surviving crew members of the *Titanic* wait to be called in for questioning by the board of inquiry.

CHAPTER FOURTEEN

"Second, to Second Officer Lightoller and his ship's crew, who did their duty as if similar occurrences were matters of daily routine; and thirdly, to the women who showed no signs of fear or panic whatsoever under conditions more appalling than were ever recorded before in the history of disasters at sea."

＊＊＊

Sadly, the Colonel did not live to see his book come out. He suffered from diabetes, and the exposure he endured during the night the *Titanic* sank and the time he spent in the freezing seas led to a decline in his health. He died on December 4, 1912. Many *Titanic* survivors attended his funeral.

In reporting Colonel Gracie's death the following day, the *New York Times* noted that, "The events of the night of the wreck were constantly on his mind. The manuscript of his work on the subject had finally been completed and sent to the printers when his last illness came. In his last hours the memories of the disaster did not leave him. Rather they crowded thicker, and he was heard to say:

"'We must get them into the boats. We must get them all into the boats.'"

＊＊＊

The *Titanic* disaster shocked people all over the globe. Jack Thayer put it this way: "To my mind the world of today awoke April 15, 1912." From that day on, the *Titanic* has continued to be part of popular culture, through fiction and nonfiction books, films, songs, undersea explorations, museum exhibitions, and the Internet.

The events of the *Titanic* disaster can be seen as a symbol of what happens through overconfidence in technology, complacence, and a mindset of profits over people's safety. The tragedy also reveals much about the society and class structure of the time. While the formal findings did not conclude that third class passengers were the victims of intentional discrimination, the statistics of the disaster, where more people in third class died than in any other, tell a more sobering story. In some cases, entire families — mothers, fathers, and children — in third class, perished.

Most of all, the *Titanic* and the questions it raises reminds us that history isn't about learning names, events, and dates. Knowing that the *Titanic* sank at 2:20 a.m. on April 15, 1912, doesn't begin to convey what happened that night and why, more than a century later, we're still drawn to this event.

We can never really know what it was like to be there when 1,496 men, women, and children perished in the icy black waters of the Atlantic.

But through the voices of survivors, we can begin to imagine how desperately Marconi operator Jack Phillips worked in those final hours, feel Charlotte Collyer's pain as she said good-bye to her beloved husband, and picture the despair on Thomas Andrews's face the moment he saw water pouring in and realized that this incredible ship — and so many on board her — was doomed.

217

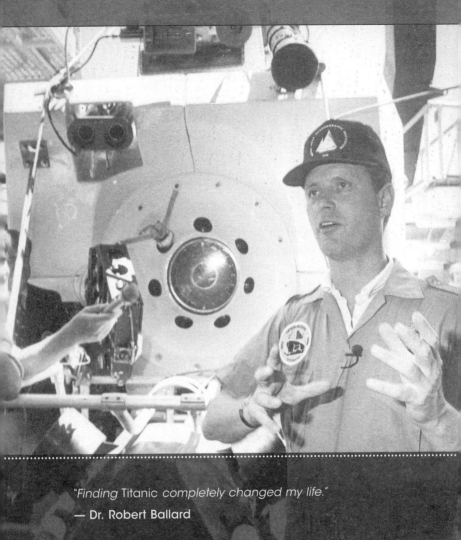

Dr. Robert Ballard led the team that discovered the wreck of the *Titanic*.

"*Finding* Titanic *completely changed my life.*"
— Dr. Robert Ballard

DISCOVERING
THE *TITANIC*

On September 1, 1985, at 1:05 a.m., a geologist and marine scientist named Dr. Robert Ballard, who had been interested in locating the *Titanic* for many years, first sighted the wreckage of the ship after a search of fifty-six days.

He and his team from the Woods Hole Oceanographic Institution were using a camera system called Argo. Argo is a device that can be towed from a remotely operated underwater vehicle; Argo enables researchers to use real-time video cameras to see underwater images.

The video cameras showed "images of twisted railing and crumpled steel." Suddenly the reality of what they were seeing struck everyone watching.

"Then it hit us, and the room fell silent. Here lay the remains of one of the greatest maritime disasters of the 20th century. We went outside to quietly honor the ship. Then we went back to work," said Ballard.

The researchers spent four days working around the clock to take photographs of the wreckage. They made important discoveries. On their last day, notes Ballard, the team was able to identify "the stern section, lying in a heap and turned in the opposite direction of the bow, which lay nearly 2,000 feet away."

Almost a year later, in July 1986, Ballard and his team returned to the site with the manned submersible *Alvin*. It took two and a half hours to descend the 12,500 feet to the bottom of the ocean. On July 13, 1986, Robert Ballard, Ralph Hollis, and

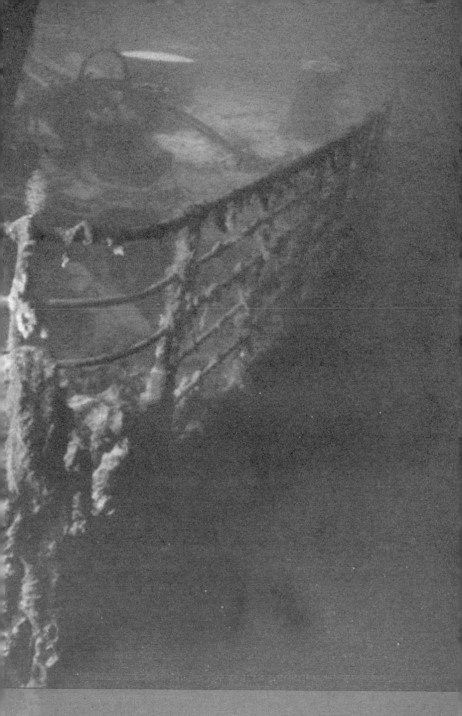
The bow of the wrecked *Titanic*.

EPILOGUE

Dudley Foster became the first human beings to set eyes on the *Titanic* since the early morning hours of April 15, 1912. In all, the team made eleven exploratory dives that year. Dr. Ballard saw china cups, huge chunks of twisted metal, and the head of a child's doll.

"Before leaving the wreck we placed two plaques on her remains," wrote Ballard. "One on the stern, honoring those who had died, and one on the bow, asking that the ship be left in peace."

Since then, the United States Congress passed the R.M.S. Titanic Maritime Memorial Act of 1986, calling for guidelines for the recovery of artifacts. A company called RMS Titanic, Inc. was granted salvage rights. According to their website, the company has conducted seven research and recovery expeditions since 1987, and recovered over fifty-five hundred objects from the site. Photographers and filmmakers, including James Cameron, who made the 1997 film *Titanic*, have also visited the wreck in recent years. The results have been used for films as well as technical research and analysis of damage to the ship.

It seems that the story of the *Titanic*, the most magnificent ship in the world, truly will go on.

⇻ GLOSSARY ⇺

able seaman: An experienced deckhand capable of performing routine duties on board a ship.

aft: Near, toward, or in the stern of a ship.

boiler: A furnace in which coal was burned to boil water and create the steam that powered the *Titanic*'s engines.

bow: The forward (or front) part of a ship.

bridge: A raised platform or structure where the Wheelhouse is mounted; the ship is navigated from here.

bulkhead: An upright partition or wall dividing a ship into compartments that help protect it by adding structural rigidity and preventing the spread of leaks, water, or fire.

collapsible: A boat made with canvas sides that can be raised and lowered so the boat can be stored flat. The collapsible boats on the *Titanic* were made by the Engelhardt company and were sometimes called "Engelhardt collapsibles."

crow's nest: A lookout platform mounted high on a ship's mast.

davit: A cranelike device, usually mounted in pairs, that can be swung over the side of a ship to lower a lifeboat or to load cargo.

forepeak: The narrow part of a vessel's bow, or the hold within it.

forward: At, near, or toward the bow of a ship.

glory hole: The traditional name for the stewards' and stokers' quarters on board a ship.

growler: A small iceberg. "A growler is really the worst form of ice. It is a larger berg melted down, or I might say a solid body of ice which is lower down to the water and more difficult to see than field ice, pack ice, floe ice, or icebergs." — Charles Herbert Lightoller, British Wreck Commissioner's Inquiry, Day 11, 13560.

hold: A storage space usually located at the bottom of a ship.

keel: The main structural element of a ship, which runs lengthwise along the center of its bottom from bow to stern and to which the frames or ribs are attached.

knot: A unit of speed equivalent to one nautical mile per hour or approximately 1.150 overland miles (6,076 feet) per hour.

port: The left side of a ship when one is on board and facing the bow.

RMS: Royal Mail Ship (or Steamer).

starboard: The right side of a ship when one is on board and facing the bow.

stern: The rear part of a ship.

stokers: Stokers and firemen both shoveled coal to feed a ship's boilers, but the position of a stoker was considered more important than that of a fireman.

tender: A boat used for transportation between a ship and the shore.

tonnage: A measure of the size or cargo-carrying capacity of a ship.

For more nautical definitions visit the Nautical Dictionary at Mystic Seaport: The Museum of America and the Sea: www .mysticseaport.org/index.cfm?fuseaction=home.viewPage&page_ id=5E023867-65B8-D398-7B2E90D4A0DC4941 or The Dictionary of English Nautical Language at www.seatalk.info.

⇻ PEOPLE IN THIS BOOK ⇺

Rhoda Abbott

Often known as "Rosa," Rhoda Abbott was the only woman plucked from the water by a lifeboat (Collapsible A). A divorced mother of two sons, the thirty-nine-year-old Rhoda supported her boys by sewing. Originally from England, she had lived in both Great Britain and Providence, Rhode Island. She refused to get into a lifeboat because her children, Rossmore and Eugene, would not be allowed in. Her sons were separated from her when the ship went down and perished. Only Rossmore's body was recovered. Rhoda spent more than two weeks hospitalized after arriving in America. She never recovered from the loss of her children and died in London, lonely and poor, on February 18, 1946.

Olaus Jorgensen Abelseth

Twenty-five years old at the time of the disaster, third class passenger Olaus ("Ole") hailed from Norway. As a teenager, he immigrated to America with his brother and worked as a farmhand. In 1908 he was homesteading on a farm in South Dakota. Ole spent the winter of 1912 visiting family in Norway and was returning to the United States on the *Titanic* along with several relatives and friends. Ole survived by swimming to Collapsible A. The two girls in his party were rescued, but Ole was the only male to survive. He married Anna Grinde in 1915, worked his farm for thirty years, and had four children. He died December 4, 1980, at the age of ninety-four.

John Jacob Astor IV

One of the richest men in America, John Jacob Astor IV was forty-seven at the time of the disaster. He was returning to the United States with his eighteen-year-old second wife, the former Madeleine Force, and their Airedale, Kitty. Colonel Astor, who had served in the Spanish-American War, was the great-grandson of John Jacob Astor, the fur trader who built one of America's greatest fortunes and for whom the city of Astoria, Oregon, is named. Madeleine escaped in Lifeboat 4, but Astor died in the sinking. Four months later, on August 14, 1912, Madeleine gave birth to a son and named him after his father.

Lawrence Beesley

Born in England in 1877, second class passenger and science teacher Lawrence Beesley sailed on the *Titanic* to visit his brother in Canada. A widower with a young son, Alec, Beesley was rescued in Lifeboat 13. He wrote a book about his experiences entitled *The Loss of the S.S. Titanic: Its Story and Its Lessons*. His son, Alec, later married Dodie Smith, who wrote many books including *The Hundred and One Dalmations*. Lawrence remarried in 1919 and had three more children. There is a well-known story that on the movie set of *A Night to Remember* (1958), Beesley attempted to enter the action and "go down with the ship" but was stopped by the director.

Joseph Boxhall

Joseph Boxhall, twenty-eight years old, was fourth officer on the *Titanic*. He came from a seafaring family and joined his first ship at the age of fifteen. He began working for the White Star Line in 1907 and met Charles Lightoller while serving on the *Oceanic*. He served in the Royal Navy Reserve during World War I and then returned to the White Star Line. Boxhall agreed to serve as a technical advisor for the 1958 film *A Night to Remember*. He died on April 25, 1967, and, according to his wishes, his ashes were scattered where he believed the ship had gone down. Joseph Boxhall's voice can be heard in a BBC interview in 1962 at www.bbc.co.uk/archive/titanic/5049.shtml.

Harold Bride

Twenty-two-year-old Harold Bride of London was the junior wireless operator on the *Titanic*. He had completed his training as a Marconi operator in July 1911. He and senior wireless operator Jack Phillips were employed by the Marconi company. Bride managed to escape on Collapsible B but suffered injuries to his feet from the cold and his position on the lifeboat. He survived and, while on board the *Carpathia*, helped operator Harold Cottam send personal messages from survivors. After the disaster, he continued to work as a wireless operator. He married in 1919 and had three children; his son was named Jack. Bride was deeply affected by the disaster and the death of Jack Phillips and it is said that he moved to Scotland to avoid the celebrity that came with his survivor status. Harold Bride died in 1956 at the age of sixty-six.

Margaret ("Molly") Brown

Margaret Brown was born in Missouri in 1867 and later moved to Colorado, where she married Joseph ("J.J.") Brown, who eventually became a rich and successful miner. A supporter of women's rights, she ran for the U.S. Senate before women had the right to vote. She became chair of the survivor's committee of the *Titanic* and continued to raise funds for victims of the disaster and speak out on issues close to her heart including education, women's rights, and labor rights. The nickname "Unsinkable Molly Brown" came about after her death in 1932.

Francis (Father Frank) Browne

Frank Browne was born in Cork, Ireland, on July 3, 1880, making him almost thirty-two at the time of the *Titanic*'s sailing. He began studying to be a Jesuit priest in 1897, was ordained in 1915, and served in World War I as a chaplain. Father Browne was injured five times during his war service. A dedicated photographer, he is most famous for the photographs he took during the first days of the *Titanic*'s voyage before he departed at Queenstown, but by the end of his life he had collected nearly 42,000 photographs. He died in July 1960. His photographs and more information on Father Browne can be found at: www.titanicphotographs.com.

Charlotte Collyer

Thirty-one-year-old Charlotte Collyer traveled on the *Titanic* with her husband, Harvey, and eight-year-old daughter, Marjorie. She and her daughter were rescued in Lifeboat 14, but her husband died in the sinking. Everything Charlotte had was wiped out in the disaster, and she received some relief funds. Although Charlotte returned to England and remarried, she died from tuberculosis just two years later. Marjorie was sent to live with her uncle in Surrey until she married in 1927. She died in 1965.

May Futrelle

Lily May Futrelle, age thirty-five, of Scituate, Massachusetts, was traveling in first class with her husband, Jacques, who was a newspaper reporter and science fiction novelist. The couple had been traveling in Europe for several weeks while their children remained at home. May was rescued in Collapsible D, but her husband perished in the sinking. She died on October 29, 1967, at the age of ninety-one.

Frank Goldsmith

Nine-year-old Frank "Frankie" Goldsmith, from Strood, Kent, in England, was traveling third class with his parents. After the sinking, in which his father was lost, he and his mother settled near Detroit, Michigan. Frank married, and he and his wife, Vickie, had three children. He ran a photo supply store. Frank's memoirs of the disaster, Titanic *Eyewitness: My Story,* were published in April 2007 by the *Titanic* Historical Society. Frank died on January 27, 1982.

Colonel Archibald Gracie

Archibald Gracie, born on January 17, 1859, was part of a wealthy New York family. A graduate of the U.S. Military Academy at West Point, Gracie had just completed a book about the Civil War and was returning from a vacation in Europe when he boarded the *Titanic* as a first class passenger. He survived by swimming to Collapsible B. Almost immediately after the sinking, Gracie began working on an account of the disaster, entitled *The Truth About the* Titanic, which was published in 1913. Gracie himself did not live to see its publication. He died on December 4, 1912, apparently of complications from diabetes. It is also thought that his health suffered because of the exposure he underwent the night of the sinking.

Henry Harper

Aged forty-eight, Henry Harper was a first class passenger on his way home to New York. He was the grandson of Joseph Harper, one of the founders of a major American publishing firm. He was traveling with his wife, Myra; a young Egyptian servant and guide from Cairo named

Hammad Hassab; and the family's Pekinese, Sun Yat-Sen. The entire party, including the dog, were rescued in Lifeboat 3. Henry Harper returned to the family business and died on March 1, 1944.

Esther and Eva Hart

Esther Hart was traveling with her seven-year-old daughter, Eva, and husband, Benjamin, to Canada in second class. Eva and her mother were rescued in Lifeboat 14, but Benjamin perished. Following their arrival in New York, they returned to England, where Eva had been born. Esther Hart remarried, and died when Eva was twenty-three. Eva was an active *Titanic* survivor, speaking out about her strong memories of hearing the screams of the victims and about the lack of lifeboats. To listen to a BBC radio interview with Eva Hart that aired on April 11, 1987, go to www.bbc.co.uk/archive/titanic/5058.shtml. Eva died in 1996 at the age of ninety-one.

Samuel Hemming

Lamp trimmer Samuel Hemming, gone to sea at age fifteen, had been working for the White Star Line for about five years. Forty-three at the time of the disaster, he served as a lamp trimmer on board the ship. Hemming assisted with the loading of lifeboats and was plucked from the water by Lifeboat 4. He died in 1928.

J. Bruce Ismay

Joseph Bruce Ismay, the son of Thomas Henry Ismay, owner of the White Star Line, was born in England in 1862. He began working for the White Star Line as an apprentice and also served as the company agent in New York. Married in 1888, he and his wife had four children. After several years in New York, he returned to England in 1891 and became a partner in the firm. When his father died in 1899, he became managing director of the company, which eventually became part of J. P. Morgan's International Mercantile Maritime Company (IMM). Sometime in 1907, Ismay and Lord Pirrie, a partner in the Belfast ship-building firm of Harland and Wolff, decided to build the Olympic class of ships, more luxurious than anything existing at the time. Ismay made a practice of going on the maiden voyage of his ships. At the time of the *Titanic*'s sinking, he famously jumped into Collapsible C, for which he was widely criticized at the time. In 1913, Ismay resigned from the company and largely withdrew from public life.

Violet Jessop

Born in 1887 in Argentina, where her Irish parents had immigrated, Violet Jessop returned with her mother and five younger siblings to Great Britain after her father's death. The eldest of six children, Violet left school to become a stewardess to help support the family. She served on three White Star Line ships — first on the *Olympic*, then on the *Titanic*'s maiden voyage, and lastly on the *Britannic*. She was rescued in Lifeboat 16. During World War I, she served as a nurse and was on board the *Titanic*'s sister ship, the *Britannic*, when it was sunk in 1916. She died in 1971.

Charles Joughin

Chief baker on the *Titanic*, Charles Joughin was born in Liverpool on August 3, 1878. He had served on the *Olympic* before joining the *Titanic*, where he had thirteen bakers working under him. He reported to the British Wreck Commissioner's Inquiry that he sent thirteen men up with four loaves of bread each to put in the lifeboats after the collision. Joughin is known for his extraordinary survival story; he claimed to be in the water for over two hours. Although he reported that he had a "drop" of liquor in his cabin, in the film *A Night to Remember* he is shown as being drunk, providing comic relief. Joughin was eventually rescued in Collapsible B. He continued to work on ships and died on December 9, 1956.

Charles Herbert Lightoller

Thirty-eight-year-old Second Officer Charles Herbert Lightoller was the most senior surviving officer of the *Titanic*. He went to sea at age thirteen, and by twenty-one had already survived a shipwreck and a cyclone. He took a break from the sea for adventures that included prospecting for gold in the Klondike and being a cowboy in Canada, then joined the White Star Line in 1900. Lightoller took an active role in helping to load the lifeboats, and as the ship was sinking, was able to save himself on Collapsible B. He served as commander of a destroyer in World War I. "Lights," as he was nicknamed, died on December 8, 1952. His voice can be heard in a 1936 interview with the BBC at: www .bbc.co.uk/archive/titanic/5047.shtml.

Harold G. Lowe

Fifth Officer Harold Lowe, age twenty-nine, had been at sea since he ran away from home at the age of fourteen. Originally from Wales, he had been with the White Star Line for a little more than a year; this was his first North Atlantic crossing. After the *Titanic* struck the iceberg, Lowe was in charge of Lifeboat 14, and kept five lifeboats together and organized a party to return to the site where the ship had sunk to search for survivors. Lowe was married in 1913 and the couple had two children. He continued his career at sea and was made a commander in the Royal Naval Reserve in World War I. He died on May 12, 1944.

Pierre Maréchal

A twenty-eight-year-old Frenchman who boarded the *Titanic* as a first class passenger at Cherbourg on April 10, Pierre Maréchal was a businessman who was playing cards with friends in the Café Parisien when the collision took place. He was rescued in Lifeboat 7. Along with two other French survivors, Alfred Omont and Paul Chevré, he wrote an account of his experiences, which was sent to France for publication. In it he said that the only item he had saved was a Sherlock Holmes book. Helen Bishop, another passenger in Lifeboat 7, is reported to have said that Monsieur Maréchal never removed his monocle, even while rowing.

Ernst Persson

Ernst Persson was a twenty-five-year-old chauffeur from Stockholm, Sweden, traveling to the United States as a third class passenger. He escaped in Lifeboat 15, but his sister, Elna Strom, and two-year-old niece, Telma (sometimes spelled "Selma"), who had been visiting family in Sweden, were lost in the sinking. Ernst moved to Indiana, where he lived with his widowed brother-in-law, Wilhelm, and became a bricklayer. His wife and children joined him later in 1912. Ernst Persson, who changed his last name to "Pearson," died on October 17, 1951.

Arthur H. Rostron

Nearly forty-three, Arthur Rostron had already been at sea for thirty years. He went to work for the Cunard Line in 1895, subsequently serving on several different ships. In January 1912, he was given command of the *Carpathia*, which regularly traveled between New York and Italy. Awakened by wireless operator Harold Cottam, Rostron immediately went to the *Titanic*'s aid, becoming one of the heroes of the disaster. He later received a silver cup from the survivors and was invited to the White House to meet President Taft. He continued to command Cunard ships, served as a ship captain for troop and hospital ships in World War I, and in 1926 was named a Knight Commander of the Order of the British Empire. He retired in 1931 and died in 1940 at the age of seventy-one.

Elizabeth Shutes

Forty-year-old Elizabeth Shutes (her name is also sometimes spelled "Shute") from New York was traveling on the *Titanic* as a governess to first class passenger Margaret Graham. Elizabeth was rescued from Lifeboat 3. Her personal account of the sinking was included in Colonel Gracie's book. She died in 1949.

E. J. Smith

Born in England in 1850, sixty-two-year-old Edward John Smith, the *Titanic*'s captain, began his sea career at the age of thirteen. He had been with the White Star Line since 1880, and received his first command seven years later at the age of thirty-seven. The most popular White Star captain, he was a natural to be chosen to command the *Titanic* on her maiden voyage. Captain Smith was last seen on the bridge of the *Titanic*.

Jack Thayer

Seventeen at the time of the sinking, high-school student Jack Thayer traveled in first class with his parents, John B. and Marian Thayer. Separated from them, he managed to survive by leaping from the ship and swimming to Collapsible B. His father, a vice president of the Pennsylvania Railroad, perished, but Jack was reunited with his mother on board the *Carpathia*. He went on to graduate from the University of

Pennsylvania, married, and had two sons. He later became vice president and treasurer of the university. After the death of his son Edward in World War II, Jack Thayer apparently became deeply depressed. He took his own life in September 1945.

Hugh Woolner

A London businessman in his forties and first class passenger on the *Titanic*, Hugh Woolner was in the first class smoking room along with Mauritz Björnström-Steffansson at the time of the collision, and the two later helped the officers and crew load the lifeboats with women and children. He and Björnström-Steffansson were both rescued by jumping into Collapsible D as it was being lowered. Hugh Woolner died on February 13, 1925.

Information on passengers and crew is drawn primarily from *Encyclopedia Titanica* and from the Titanic Inquiry Project. To learn more about all the survivors and victims, visit www.encyclopedia-titanica.org.

⇢ OTHER FAMOUS *TITANIC* FIGURES ⇠

In addition to those whose stories appear in this book, other passengers and crew members have become well known in *Titanic* history. They include:

Millvina (Elizabeth Gladys) Dean was the last survivor of the *Titanic* to die. Born on February 2, 1912, she was only nine weeks old when her parents, Bertram and Georgette Dean, left England to move to Kansas with their new baby girl and son, Bertram, who was almost two. Millvina's father died in the sinking. Her mother was able to raise Millvina and her brother in part thanks to *Titanic* relief funds. Millvina, who never married, retired to Southampton and became a *Titanic* celebrity in her seventies, giving interviews and going to conventions. She died on May 31, 2009, at the age of ninety-seven.

Sir Cosmo and Lady Duff Gordon became infamous for being in Lifeboat 1, which was lowered with only twelve people and which made no effort to save others. Cosmo Duff Gordon had married Lucy (known as "Lucile") Wallace, a divorced dressmaker and fashion designer, in 1900. After the disaster, fireman Charles Hendrickson testified that both Sir Cosmo and Lady Duff Gordon said they should not go back to help others because it would be too dangerous.

The Duff Gordons were the only passengers called to testify in the British Inquiry. In one exchange, Lady Duff Gordon was asked if she knew that there were people in the *Titanic* as the ship was sinking. "'No, I did not think so; I do not think I was thinking anything about it'" was her reply. Her husband's answers were equally callous. When asked at the British Inquiry if he thought about whether or not the boat could save some of the people in the water, he answered, "'I was not thinking about it. At that time I was attending to my wife, as I think I said just now. We had had rather a serious evening, you know.'" Cosmo Duff Gordon died in 1931, and Lady Duff Gordon died in 1935.

Benjamin Guggenheim, forty-six, was an American millionaire and mining tycoon. He gave *Titanic* steward James Etches a written message for his wife that read, "If anything should happen to me, tell my wife in New York that I've done my best in doing my duty." He and his secretary discarded warm sweaters and were seen dressed in evening clothes the night of the sinking. Guggenheim is also reported to have said, "We've dressed up in our best and are prepared to go down like gentlemen." He died when the *Titanic* sank and his body was not recovered. Guggenheim was traveling with his mistress, twenty-four-year-old French singer, Léontine Aubart. Ms. Aubart wrote to the White Star Line asking for reimbursement for clothing and jewelry she had lost, including twenty-four pairs of shoes, twenty-four night costumes of silk and lace, twenty-four dresses and wraps, a tiara, seven hats, and one gold bag with sapphires.

Wallace Henry Hartley, age thirty-three, was born in England, where he became a violinist. He was the band leader on the *Titanic* and traveled second class. He became famous for leading his musicians in ragtime tunes after the collision until almost the end. People interested in the *Titanic* still debate and wonder what was the band's final song; some passengers recall hearing "Nearer My God to Thee," while other eyewitnesses such as Harold Bride remember hearing "Songe d'Automne." Wallace Hartley and the other seven members of the *Titanic*'s orchestra died in the sinking.

Edmond and Michel Navratil, ages two and three, were known as the "orphans of the *Titanic*." Their French father had taken his sons away from his estranged wife and was traveling under an assumed name. The boys were rescued in Collapsible D, but their father died in the sinking. The boys spoke no English, and on the *Carpathia* they were not claimed. First class passenger Margaret Hays volunteered to take care of them until family could be found. Their mother recognized their picture after newspaper stories were published proclaiming, "Tots Saved from the Sea." The White Star Line paid for her to travel to America in May to be reunited with her boys. Edmond died in 1953, and Michel died in 2001 at the age of ninety-two.

Ida and Isidor Straus were first class passengers who became famous for their devotion to each other and their decision to stay together when the *Titanic* sank. Mr. Isidor Straus, who was sixty-seven, had come to America as a boy of nine. He and his brother were in the dry goods business and became co-owners of R. H. Macy and Company in 1896. Isidor's wife, Ida, age sixty-three, almost boarded Lifeboat 8. She was overheard to say, "'We have lived together for many years. Where you go, I go.'" Although Colonel Archibald Gracie and some of her other friends tried to persuade her to get into a lifeboat, the couple stayed together and sat on deck chairs. Both were lost in the sinking. Their memorial service in New York was attended by 40,000 people.

Information on these passengers and crew members is drawn primarily from *Encyclopedia Titanica*, www.encyclopedia-titanica.org, and from the Titanic Inquiry Project.

SURVIVOR LETTERS FROM THE *CARPATHIA*

On the waves of the Atlantic 16th

Dear Mother and Sister,
I will now briefly write a few words to you to let you know that I am alive after great suffering and difficulties. You have probably read in the newspaper that the ship we travelled on sank. Oh great God what I have suffered on this voyage. . . . I feel so strange I can hardly write, I can't collect my thoughts. I have bad news to tell . . . They were lowering lifeboats and I was thrown into one of them. I held on to Nils [her fiancé] with one hand and wanted to take him along, but they held him, being afraid that there would be too many of us. I screamed as loud as I could and wanted to go back, but at the same time I was lowered . . ."

— *Olga Lundin, second class passenger*

On board the Carpathia

Thursday, 18th April, 1912
I think we all feel a little better this morning, We, that are so fortunate, having lost no one; but all the poor women's faces are piteous to see; yesterday morning I was very busy . . . cutting out garments for the Steerage and Second Class children, some of whom had no clothes at all, we made little coats and leggings out of the blankets . . . I slept a little better, but one wakens terrified, which is very silly, as we have nothing to grumble

at in comparison with the poor widows, Oh, it is too dreadful to see them . . ."

— Gladys Cherry, first class passenger

Dear Mother,
I am saved, but I have lost everything. I must, how-ever, be thankful for my life. I have not a penny and no clothes. I was thrown on board a little boat in my nightdress and boots. I had no stockings on. We were in this little boat in the middle of the ocean for six hours, and I was nearly frozen when we were picked up. . . . We could hear the screams from the men as the Titanic was sinking. I think there are hundreds drowned. . . . I don't know what I shall do when I get to New York . . . I am frightened to death nearly . . .
Your loving daughter,
"Maud"

— Maude Sincock, second class passenger

Our ship struck an iceberg. I went on deck and met a sailor who asked me to help lower the boats. The sailor said, 'Take a chance yourself.' I did, as did my friend, but the officers came along and ordered us off the boat. A woman said, 'Lay down, lad, you are somebody's child.' She put a rug over me and the boat went out, so I was saved. I'll write you a note when I get to New York.

— Daniel Buckley, third class passenger

Wednesday, Carpathia

Just another line to say I am very well and getting quite used to things now . . . I escaped in my night-dress and coat and petticoats; everything else has gone . . . We are sleeping like a lot of dead things all over the floors of the ship . . . I dare say you all have lots of sympathy for me, but believe me, I am one of the lucky ones. My life is saved, my health is not impaired, and I have not lost anyone belonging to me. I tell you I have lots to be thankful for. I was ready to go down with the ship but they forced me into the lifeboat. I think it wicked to save the single girls, but now that I saved a baby whose mother was in another boat I don't mind. We are still very fog bound, which makes all very anxious to arrive in New York.

— Edwina Trout, second class passenger

For more letters of survivors, see *On Board RMS* Titanic: *Memories of the Maiden Voyage*, by George Behe, Lulu.com: 2011.

⇒ *TITANIC* TIMELINE ⇐

(In some cases, times cited are approximate)

Tuesday, April 2

6:00 a.m.   *Titanic* begins sea trials.

8:00 p.m.   *Titanic* leaves Belfast for Southampton.

Wednesday, April 3

Titanic reaches Southampton around midnight.

Friday, April 5

Titanic is "dressed" with flags.

Saturday, April 6

Recruitment day for most of the crew; cargo begins to arrive.

Monday, April 8

Much of the fresh food is brought on board.

Wednesday, April 10

12:00 p.m.   *Titanic* sets sail on her maiden voyage.

6:30 p.m.–8:00 p.m.

Titanic anchors at Cherbourg, France, to load passengers.

Thursday, April 11

11:30 a.m.–1:30 p.m.

Titanic anchors at Queenstown to pick up more passengers; Father Frank Browne leaves the ship.

Sunday, April 14

Ice warnings are received throughout the day.

11:40 p.m.   Lookout Frederick Fleet spots an iceberg.

| 11:50 p.m. | In the first 10 minutes, water rises about 14 feet above the keel. The first five compartments take on water. |

Monday, April 15

12:00 a.m.	Thomas Andrews tells Captain Smith the ship is doomed.
12:15 a.m.	Ships begin to receive the *Titanic*'s distress signals.
12:40 a.m.	Lifeboat 7 on starboard side is the first boat launched, with 27 or 28 people — less than half its capacity of 65.
1:00 a.m.	Lifeboat 8 is the first boat launched from port side.
2:20 a.m.	*Titanic* sinks.
4:10 a.m.	*Carpathia* picks up the first lifeboat.
8:50 a.m.	*Carpathia* leaves the site for New York.

Thursday, April 18

| 9:00 p.m. | *Carpathia* arrives in New York. |

April 19–May 25

United States Senate Inquiry hearings

May 28

United States Senate Inquiry Report

May 2–July 3

British Wreck Commissioner's Inquiry hearings

July 30

British Wreck Commissioner's Report

BE A *TITANIC* RESEARCHER:
❖ FIND OUT MORE ❖

The whole truth about the *Titanic* will never be known. There are conflicting stories of survivors, differing eyewitness versions of what happened, and gaps in knowledge. Some of the key people — the captain, the designer, the chief engineer, and the officer on the bridge at the time of the collision, did not survive to give evidence. Investigators at the time did not have access to the actual location of the wreck. Maybe that's part of what has fascinated us about the disaster for the past century.

Today, you can find articles on how the ship sank; you can compare notes with other amateur researchers and *Titanic* experts on passengers and their stories; and you can debate the precise timeline of events. On the next page are some links to actual voices of *Titanic* eyewitnesses and questions to get you started. Check out the bibliography for more books, articles, and websites.

A great place to start is with the testimony of people who were there. You can find the official British and American inquiry hearings on the Titanic Inquiry Project website at www.titanicinquiry.org. You can also find out more about passengers and crew — and just about everything else about the *Titanic* on the Encyclopedia Titanica website at www.encyclopedia-titanica.org.

Listen to voices from the *Titanic* at the BBC Archive.

Fourth Officer Joseph Boxhall
www.bbc.co.uk/archive/titanic/5049.shtml

Second Officer Charles Herbert Lightoller
www.bbc.co.uk/archive/titanic/5047.shtml

Survivor Eva Hart
www.bbc.co.uk/archive/titanic/5058.shtml

Some Questions for *Titanic* Researchers

- Chief Baker Joughin claims to have spent over two hours in the water. What do you think?

- People have been arguing about the *Californian* and her captain, Stanley Lord, for years. Was Captain Lord at fault?

- Very few of the *Titanic* lifeboats went back to the ship. What would you have done?

- What exactly caused the *Titanic* to sink and what kind of damage did she sustain?

- Why do you think Captain Smith did not slow down on Sunday, April 14, 1912, despite receiving warnings of ice ahead?

- What exactly did First Officer William Murdoch do on the bridge in the moments before and after the iceberg was sighted?

- What would it be like to be a wireless operator on the night of the disaster? Would it have made a difference if Jack Phillips and Harold Bride had taken the *Mesaba*'s ice message to the bridge?

- For years, people thought that the *Carpathia* was fifty-eight nautical miles away from the *Titanic*. But when the *Titanic* was discovered in 1985, it turns out the wreck was thirteen nautical miles south and east of her SOS position. How did Captain Rostron find the lifeboats?

⇝ *TITANIC* FACTS AND FIGURES ⇜

Length... 882½ feet

Number of propellers 3

Number of watertight bulkheads 15

Number of lifeboats 20

Date work began .... March 31, 1909

Launch date .... May 31, 1911

Sea trial date .... April 2, 1912

Maiden voyage date........................... April 10, 1912

Cost to build .... $7.5 million

Number of funnels 4

Number of boilers 29

Number of masts 2

Gross registered tonnage 46,239

Radio call sign.. MGY

Number of life belts............................. 3,560

Total passenger and crew capacity.................. 3,547

Total passenger and crew head count............. 2,208

Number of bodies later found 338

Depth of the wreck .... 12,460 feet

Date of wreck discovery .... September 1, 1985

Date of the first dive to the wreck........................ July 13, 1986

FROM THE BRITISH WRECK COMMISSIONER'S FINAL REPORT, 1912

AUTHOR'S NOTE: On July 30, 1912, the British Wreck Commissioner's Inquiry Report was released. It included an account of the damage to the ship from the water, based on the testimony of witnesses. Today researchers continue to debate this same testimony to try to learn as much as possible about what happened after the ship struck an iceberg on the night of April 14, 1912.

Description of the Damage to the Ship and its Gradual Final Effect

Extent of the Damage

The collision with the iceberg, which took place at 11.40 p.m., caused damage to the bottom of the starboard side of the vessel at about 10 feet above the level of the keel, but there was no damage above this height. There was damage in: The forepeak, No. 1 hold, No. 2 hold, No. 3 hold, No. 6 boiler room, No. 5 boiler room.

The damage extended over a length of about 300 ft.

Time in which the Damage was Done

As the ship was moving at over 20 knots, she would have passed through 300 ft. in less than 10 seconds, so that the damage was done in about this time.

Flooding in the First Ten Minutes

In **No. 1 hold** there was 7 ft. of water.

In **No. 2 hold** five minutes after the collision water was seen rushing in at the bottom of the firemen's passage on the starboard side, so that the ship's side was damaged abaft of bulkhead B sufficiently to open the side of the firemen's passage, which was 3½ feet from the outer skin of the ship, thereby flooding both the hold and the passage.

In **No. 3 hold** the mail room was filled soon after the collision. The floor of the mail room is 24 feet above the keel.

In **No. 6 boiler room**, when the collision took place, water at once poured in at about 2 feet above the stokehold plates, on the starboard side, at the after end of the boiler room.

Some of the firemen immediately went through the watertight door opening to No. 5 boiler room because the water was flooding the place. The watertight doors in the engine rooms were shut from the bridge almost immediately after the collision. Ten minutes later it was found that there was water to the height of 8 feet above the double bottom in No. 6 boiler room.

No. 5 boiler room was damaged at the ship's side in the starboard forward bunker at a distance of 2 feet above the stokehold plates, at 2 feet from the watertight bulkhead between Nos. 5 and 6 boiler rooms. Water poured in at that place as it would from an ordinary fire hose. At the time of the collision this bunker had no coal in it. The bunker door was closed when water was seen to be entering the ship.

In **No. 4 boiler room** there was no indication of any damage at the early stages of the sinking.

Gradual Effect of the Damage

It will thus be seen that all the six compartments forward of **No. 4 boiler room** were open to the sea by damage which existed at about 10 feet above the keel. At 10 minutes after the collision the water seems to have risen to about 14 feet above the keel in all these compartments except No. 5 boiler room. After the first ten minutes, the water rose steadily in all these six compartments.

The forepeak above the peak tank was not filled until an hour after the collision when the vessel's bow was submerged to above C deck. The water then flowed in from the top through the deck scuttle forward of the collision bulkhead. It was by this scuttle that access was obtained to all the decks below C down to the peak tank top on the Orlop deck.

At 12 o'clock water was coming up in **No. 1 hatch**. It was getting into the firemen's quarters and driving the firemen out. It was rushing round No. 1 hatch on G deck and coming mostly from the starboard side, so that in 20 minutes the water had risen above G deck in No. 1 hold.

In **No. 2 hold** about 40 minutes after the collision the water was coming in to the seamen's quarters on E deck through a burst fore and aft wooden bulkhead of a third class cabin opposite the seamen's wash place. Thus, the water had risen in No. 2 hold to about 3 ft. above E deck in 40 minutes.

In **No. 3 hold** the mail room was afloat about 20 minutes after the collision. The bottom of the mail room which is on the Orlop deck, is 24 feet above the keel.

The watertight doors on F deck at the fore and after ends of No. 3 compartment were not closed then.

The mail room was filling and water was within 2 ft. of G deck, rising fast, when the order was given to clear the boats.

There was then no water on F deck.

There is a stairway on the port side on G deck which leads down to the first class baggage room on the Orlop deck immediately below. There was water in this baggage room 25 minutes after the collision. Half an hour after the collision water was up to G deck in the mail room.

Thus the water had risen in this compartment to within 2 feet of G deck in 20 minutes, and above G deck in 25 to 30 minutes.

No. 6 boiler room was abandoned by the men almost immediately after the collision. Ten minutes later the water had risen to 8 feet above the top of the double bottom, and probably reached the top of the bulkhead at the after end of the compartment, at the level of E deck, in about one hour after the collision.

In **No. 5 boiler room** there was no water above the stokehold plates, until a rush of water came through the pass between the boilers from the forward end, and drove the leading stoker out.

It has already been shown in the description of what happened in the first ten minutes, that water was coming into No. 5 boiler room in the forward starboard bunker at 2 feet above the plates in a stream about the size of a deck hose. The door in this bunker had been dropped probably when water was first discovered, which was a few minutes after the collision. This would cause the water to be retained in the bunker until it rose high enough to burst the door which was weaker than the bunker bulkhead. This happened about an hour after the collision.

No. 4 boiler room. — One hour and 40 minutes after collision water was coming in forward, in No. 4 boiler room, from underneath the floor in the forward part, in small quantities. The men remained in that stokehold till ordered on deck.

Nos. 3, 2, and 1 boiler rooms. — When the men left No. 4 some of them went through Nos. 3, 2, and 1 boiler rooms into the reciprocating engine room, and from there on deck. There was no water in the boiler rooms abaft No. 4 one hour 40 minutes after the collision (1.20 a.m.), and there was then none in the reciprocating and turbine engine rooms.

Electrical engine room and tunnels. — There was no damage to these compartments.

From the foregoing it follows that there was no damage abaft No. 4 boiler room.

All the watertight doors aft of the main engine room were opened after the collision. Half an hour after the collision the watertight doors from the engine room to the stokehold were opened as far forward as they could be to No. 4 boiler room.

Final Effect of the Damage

The later stages of the sinking cannot be stated with any precision, owing to a confusion of the times which was natural under the circumstances.

The forecastle deck was not under water at 1.35 a.m. Distress signals were fired until two hours after the collision (1.45 a.m.). At this time the fore deck was under water. The forecastle head was not then submerged though it was getting close down to the water, about half an hour before she disappeared (1.50 a.m.).

When the last boat, lowered from davits (D), left the ship, A deck was under water, and water came up the stairway under the Boat deck almost immediately afterwards. After this the other port collapsible (B), which had been stowed on the officers' house, was uncovered, the lashings cut adrift, and she was swung round over the edge of the coamings of the deckhouse on to the Boat deck.

Very shortly afterwards, the vessel, according to Mr. Lightoller's account, seemed to take a dive, and he just walked into the water. When he came to the surface all the funnels were above the water.

Her stern was gradually rising out of the water, and the propellers were clear of the water. The ship did not break in two [we now know that the *Titanic* did, in fact, break apart] and she did eventually attain the perpendicular, when the second funnel from aft about reached the water. There were no lights burning then, though they kept alight practically until the last.

Before reaching the perpendicular when at an angle of 50 or 60 degrees, there was a rumbling sound which may be attributed to the boilers leaving their beds and crashing down on to or through the bulkheads. She became more perpendicular and finally absolutely perpendicular, when she went slowly down.

After sinking as far as the after part of the Boat deck she went down more quickly. The ship disappeared at 2.20 a.m.

TITANIC: THE LIFEBOAT
LAUNCHING SEQUENCE REEXAMINED

By Bill Wormstedt, Tad Fitch, and George Behe, with contributions by Sam Halpern and J. Kent Layton.

(Originally published in edited form in the "*The Titanic Commutato*r" No. 155, 2001. *Titanic* Historical Society.)

(This revised and expanded version © 2009, 2010 by Bill Wormstedt, Tad Fitch, and George Behe.)

Reprinted with permission. Available as Table 2 online in the article at: wormstedt.com/Titanic/lifeboats/lifeboats.htm.

Launch Times Re-Examined					
Port Side			Starboard Side		
Time	Boat	In Charge of Loading	Time	Boat	In Charge of Loading
12:40			12:40	7	Murdoch, Lowe
12:45			12:45	5	Murdoch, Lowe, Pitman (at 12:43)
12:47		Rockets first fired			
12:50			12:50		
12:55			12:55	3	Murdoch, Lowe
1:00	8	Lightoller, Wilde, Smith	1:00		
1:05			1:05	1	Murdoch, Lowe
1:10	6	Lightoller	1:10		
1:15			1:15		

Port Side			Starboard Side		
Time	Boat	In Charge of Loading	Time	Boat	In Charge of Loading
1:20	16	Moody	1:20		
1:25	14	Lowe, Wilde, Lightoller	1:25		
1:30	12	Wilde, Lightoller	1:30	9	Murdoch (Moody?)
1:35			1:35	11	Murdoch
1:40			1:40	13 15	Murdoch, Moody Murdoch, Moody (at 1:41)
1:45	2	Wilde, Smith	1:45		
1:50		Rockets cease firing	1:50		
1:50	10 4	Murdoch, Lightoller	1:50		
1:55			1:55		
2:00			2:00	C	Murdoch, Wilde
2:05	D	Lightoller, Wilde	2:05		
2:10			2:10		
2:15	(B)	(Lightoller) (bridge goes under)	2:15	(A)	(Murdoch, Moody) (bridge goes under)
2:20			2:20		

⇒ *TITANIC* STATISTICS: ⇐
WHO LIVED AND WHO DIED

Figures supplied by Lester J. Mitcham and used with permission.

Passengers and crew on board
when the *Titanic* left Queenstown.

Men	Lost	Saved	Total	% Saved
1st Class[1]	118	58	176	33.00%
2nd Class[1]	154	13	167	7.80%
3rd Class	392	60	452	13.30%
Men Passengers	664	131	795	16.50%
Men Crew	676	192	868	22.10%
Total Men	**1340**	**323**	**1663**	**19.40%**

Women	Lost	Saved	Total	% Saved
1st Class	4	139	143	97.20%
2nd Class	12	83	95	87.40%
3rd Class	90	91	181	50.30%
Women Passengers	106	313	419	74.70%
Women Crew	3	20	23	87.00%
Total Women	**109**	**333**	**442**	**75.30%**

Children[2]	Lost	Saved	Total	% Saved
1st Class	1	4	5	80.00%
2nd Class	-	22	22	100.00%
3rd Class	46	30	76	39.50%
Total Children	**47**	**56**	**103**	**54.40%**

Totals	Lost	Saved	Total	% Saved
1st Class	123	201	324	62.00%
2nd Class	166	118	284	41.50%
3rd Class	528	181	709	25.50%
Passengers	817	500	1317	38.00%
Crew	679	212	891	23.80%
Total On Board	**1496**	**712**	**2208**	**32.20%**

[1] 1st Class numbers include three members of the Harland & Wolff Guarantee Group. 2nd Class numbers include the other six members of the Harland & Wolff Guarantee Group and the eight bandsmen, all of whom traveled on passenger tickets. All seventeen men were lost.

[2] According to the *Titanic's Certificates for Clearance*, an adult passenger was aged "12 years and upwards."

⋟ SELECTED BIBLIOGRAPHY ⋞

Archbold, Rick. *Last Dinner on the* Titanic. Toronto: Madison Press, 1997.

Barratt, Nick. *Lost Voices from the* Titanic*: The Definitive Oral History.* New York: Palgrave Macmillan, 2010.

Beesley, Lawrence. *The Loss of the S.S.* Titanic*: Its Story and Its Lessons,* 1912. Forgotten Books, 2008. forgottenbooks.org/info/9781606800447.

Behe, George M. *On Board RMS* Titanic*: Memories of the Maiden Voyage.* Raleigh: Lulu.com, 2010.

Beveridge, Bruce et al. Titanic*: The Ship Magnificent. Volume One: Design & Construction.* Stroud, UK: History Press, 2008.

———. Titanic*: The Ship Magnificent. Volume Two: Interior Design & Fitting Out.* Stroud, UK: History Press, 2008.

Booth, John, and Sean Coughlan. Titanic*: Signals of Disaster.* Westbury, UK: White Star, 1993.

Boyd-Smith, Peter. Titanic*: From Rare Historical Reports.* Southampton: Steamship, 1994.

Brewster, Hugh, and Laurie Coulter. *882½ Amazing Answers to Your Questions About the* Titanic. New York: Scholastic, 1998.

Brown, David G. *The Last Log of the* Titanic. Camden, ME: International Marine, 2001.

Bryceson, Dave. *The* Titanic *Disaster: As Reported in the British National Press, April–July 1912.* New York: Norton, 1997.

Butler, Daniel Allen. *The Other Side of the Night: The* Carpathia, *the* Californian, *and the Night the* Titanic *Was Lost.* Drexel Hill, PA: Casemate, 2009.

———. *"Unsinkable": The Full Story of the RMS* Titanic. Cambridge, MA: Da Capo, 1998.

Eaton, John P., and Charles A. Haas. Titanic*: Triumph and Tragedy.* 2nd ed. New York: Norton, 1995.

Geller, Judith B. Titanic*: Women and Children First.* New York: Norton, 1998.

Goldsmith, Frank J. W. Titanic *Eyewitness: My Story.* Indian Orchard, MA: Titanic Historical Society, 2007.

Gracie, Archibald. Titanic*: A Survivor's Story.* Stroud, UK: History Press, 2009. First published as *The Truth About the* Titanic, 1913.

Green, Rod. *Building the* Titanic*: An Epic Tale of Human Endeavour and Modern Engineering.* London: Carlton, 2005.

Haisman, David. Titanic*: The Edith Brown Story.* Milton Keynes, UK: AuthorHouse, 2009.

Hustak, Alan. Titanic*: The Canadian Story.* Montreal: Véhicule Press, 1998.

Hutchings, David F. *RMS* Titanic*: 75 Years of Legend.* Southampton: Kingfisher, 1987.

Hyslop, Donald, Alastair Forsyth, and Sheila Jemima. Titanic *Voices: Memories from the Fateful Voyage.* New York: St. Martin's, 1994.

Jessop, Violet. Titanic *Survivor: The Newly Discovered Memoirs of Violet Jessop Who Survived Both the* Titanic *and* Britannic *Disasters.* Ed. John Maxtone-Graham. Dobbs Ferry, NY: Sheridan House, 1997.

Kuntz, Tom, ed. *The* Titanic *Disaster Hearings: The Official Transcripts of the 1912 Senate Investigation.* New York: Pocket Books, 1998.

LaRoe, Lisa Moore. Titanic*: Collector's Edition.* Washington, D.C.: National Geographic, 1999.

Lord, Walter. *The Night Lives On.* New York: Morrow, 1986.

———. *A Night to Remember.* New York: Holt, 1955.

Lynch, Don, and Ken Marschall. Titanic*: An Illustrated History.* Edison, NJ: Wellfleet, 1992.

Marcus, Geoffrey. *The Maiden Voyage.* New York: Viking, 1969.

Marschall, Ken. *Inside the* Titanic. Boston: Little, Brown, 1997.

Marshall, Logan, ed. *On Board the* Titanic*: The Complete Story with Eyewitness Accounts.* Reprint, Mineola, NY: Dover, 2006. First published as *The Sinking of the* Titanic *and Great Sea Disasters*, 1912.

Matsen, Brad. Titanic's Last Secrets. New York: Twelve, 2008.

McMillan, Beverly, and Stanley Lehrer. Titanic: Fortune and Fate: Catalogue from the Mariners' Museum Exhibition. New York: Simon & Schuster, 1998.

Merideth, Lee W. Titanic Names: A Complete List of Passengers and Crew. Sunnyvale, CA: Rocklin, 2007.

Molony, Senan. Titanic: A Primary Source History. New York: Gareth Stevens, 2006.

Mowbray, Jay Henry, ed. Sinking of the Titanic: Eyewitness Accounts. Reprint, Mineola, NY: Dover, 1998.

O'Donnell, E. E. The Last Days of the Titanic: Photographs and Mementos of the Tragic Maiden Voyage. Niwat, CO: Roberts Rinehart, 1997.

Quinn, Paul J. Dusk to Dawn: Survivor Accounts of the Last Night on the Titanic. Hollis, NH: Fantail, 1999.

———. Titanic at Two A.M.: Final Events Surrounding the Doomed Liner; An Illustrated Narrative with Survivor Accounts. Hollis, NH: Fantail, 1997.

Soderman, D. Flodin. Emma Eliza Bucknell: Titanic Survivor. Paxton, MA: Gundi, 2008.

Thayer, John B. The Sinking of the S.S. Titanic. Chicago: Academy Chicago, 1998. First printed 1940, privately.

Tibballs, Geoff, ed. The Mammoth Book of the Titanic: Contemporary Accounts from Survivors and the World's Press. New York: Carrol & Graf, 2002.

Torricelli, Robert, and Andrew Carroll, eds. In Our Own Words: Extraordinary Speeches of the American Century. New York: Kodansha America, 1999.

Wade, Wyn Craig. The Titanic: End of a Dream. New York: Penguin, 1986.

Watson, Arnold and Betty. Roster of Valor: The Titanic Halifax Legacy. Indian Orchard, MA: Titanic Historical Society, 1984.

Wels, Susan. Titanic: Legacy of the World's Greatest Ocean Liner. New York: Time-Life, 1997.

Winocour, Jack, ed. The Story of the Titanic As Told by Its Survivors. Mineola, NY: Dover, 1960.

Other Resources, Articles, and Websites

Bracken, Robert. "The Mystery of Rhoda Abbott Revealed." ET Research, 7 June 2004. www.encyclopedia-titanica.org/rhoda-abbott.html.

Brown, David G. "Chronology — Sinking of the S.S. *Titanic*." ET Research, 13 June 2009. www.encyclopedia-titanica.org/chronology-sinking-of-ss-titanic.html.

"Captain Arthur H. Rostron." *Titanic-Titanic.com*. www.titanic-titanic.com/captain_rostron.shtml.

Encyclopedia Titanica. www.encyclopedia-titanica.org.

History Channel, The. www.history.com/topics/titanic.

Kuhn, Arthur K. "International Aspects of the *Titanic* Case." *The American Journal of International Law*, 9, no. 2 (1915): 336–351. Google eBook.

Mitcham, Lester. "The Statistics of the Disaster." ET Research, 14 February 2001. www.encyclopedia-titanica.org/titanic-statistics.html.

National Maritime Museum. "The *Titanic*." www.nmm.ac.uk/explore/sea-and-ships/facts/ships-and-seafarers/the-titanic.

National Museums Northern Ireland. "*Titanic*: Stories of People, Places and Things." www.nmni.com/titanic.

National Postal Museum. "*Titanic*'s Mail." www.postalmuseum.si.edu/resources/6a2a_titanic.html.

New York Times, April 16, 1912.

New York Times, April 28, 1912.

New York Times, December 5, 1912.

Ottmers, Rob. "British Wreck Commissioner's Inquiry." Titanic *Inquiry Project*. www.titanicinquiry.org/BOTInq/BOT01.php.

Riniolo, Todd C. et al. "An Archival Study of Eyewitness Memory of the *Titanic*'s Final Plunge." *The Journal of General Psychology*, 54, no. 1 (2003): 89–95.

RMS *Titanic*, Inc. *RMS* Titanic *Home*. www.rmstitanic.net.

Stephenson, Parks. "More Questions than Answers, Part 2." Titanic Commutator 30, no. 173 (2006). Also available online at marconigraph.com/titanic/breakup/mgy_breakup.html.

"Technical Facts about the *Titanic*." Titanic *and Other White Star Line*

Ships. www.titanic-whitestarships.com/MGY_Tech_Facts.htm.

"*Titanic* Deckplans." *Encyclopedia Titanica*. www.encyclopedia-titanica
.org/deckplans.

"*Titanic* Explorer: Explore and Magnify the Ship's Deck Plans." Discovery
Channel. dsc.discovery.com/convergence/titanic/explorer/explorer
.html.

Titanic *Historical Society*. www.titanic1.org.

Titanic *Inquiry Project*. www.titanicinquiry.org.

TitanicPhotographs.com. A Collection of Images Taken by Father Frank
Browne. www.titanicphotographs.com.

Titanic-Titanic.com. www.titanic-titanic.com/index.shtml.

"United States Senate Inquiry." Titanic *Inquiry Project*. www.titanicinquiry
.org/USInq/AMInq01.php.

Worcester Telegram, April 20, 1912.

Wormstedt, Bill. "An Analysis of the Bodies Recovered from the *Titanic*,"
22 October 2000. *Bill Wormstedt's* Titanic. wormstedt.com/titanic/
analysis.html.

Wormstedt, Bill et al. "*Titanic*: The Lifeboat Launching Sequence
Re-Examined." *Bill Wormstedt's* Titanic. wormstedt.com/Titanic/
lifeboats/lifeboats.htm.

⤞ SOURCE NOTES ⤝

Chapter One

"Mummy! . . .": Goldsmith, Frank J. W., Titanic *Eyewitness: My Story Written by a Survivor in Third Class* (Indian Orchard, MA: *Titanic* Historical Society, 2007) 6.

J. Bruce Ismay: Eaton, John P., and Charles A. Haas, Titanic: *Triumph and Tragedy,* 2nd ed. (New York: Norton, 1995) 13.

Combining luxury with stability . . . : ibid.

Cost to build . . . : ibid. 21.

When the *Titanic* was registered . . . : Beveridge, Bruce et al., Titanic: *the Ship Magnificent, Volume One: Design & Construction* (Stroud, UK: History Press, 2008) 46.

Starting work at 7:50 a.m. . . . : Eaton and Haas 18.

Ten months and millions of hours . . . : Lynch, Don, and Ken Marschall, Titanic: *An Illustrated History* (Edison, NJ: Wellfleet, 1992) 25.

Anchor . . . : ibid. 21.

The *Titanic* had left Belfast . . . : Eaton and Haas 44–46.

The *Titanic* sailed with five Sea Post Office clerks . . . : National Postal Museum, "*Titanic*'s Mail," www.postalmuseum.si.edu/ resources/6a2a_titanic.html.

Crew members signed up . . . : Eaton and Haas 55.

Less than 50 . . . : David G. Brown, e-mail message to author, September 27, 2010.

Estimates based on the *Olympic* . . . : Eaton and Haas 57.

Titanic cargo list: *Titanic-Titanic.com,* www.titanic-titanic.com/ titanic_cargo_list.shtml; see also Eaton and Haas 278.

Differences in Olympic-class liners: *Titanic-titanic.com,* www .titanic-titanic.com/olympic_class_liners.shtml.

"a foul place . . .": Jessop, Violet, Titanic *Survivor: The Newly Discovered Memoires of Violet Jessop Who Survived Both the* Titanic *and* Britannic *Disasters,* John Maxtone-Graham, ed. (Dobbs Ferry, NY: Sheridan House, 1997) 117.

"His gentle face . . .": ibid.

"Often during our rounds . . .": ibid. 123.

"racks, tables, chairs . . .": Eaton and Haas 57.

"The *Titanic* is now about complete . . .": ibid.

"Life aboard . . .": Jessop 117–118.

Joe Mulholland told this tale in an interview in the *Irish Sunday Independent* (April 15, 1962). Molony, Senan, Titanic: *A Primary Source History* (New York: Gareth Stevens, 2005) 12.

"I was thoroughly familiar . . .": Winocour, Jack, ed., *The Story of the* Titanic *As Told by Its Survivors* (Mineola, NY: Dover, 1960) 275.

"With the *Titanic* . . .": ibid. 277.

"It was clear . . .": ibid.

A nest of bees . . . : ibid. 278.

"With a feeling akin . . .": O'Donnell, E. E., *The Last Days of the* Titanic: *Photographs and Mementos of the Tragic Maiden Voyage* (Niwot, CO: Roberts Rinehart, 1997) 93.

"A voice beside me . . .": ibid. 94.

and break a sort of suction . . . : David G. Brown, e-mail message to author, February 12, 2011.

Near-collision with the *New York*: Eaton and Haas 76–77.

Three first class passengers: Lester Mitcham, e-mail message to author, February 18, 2011.

Passenger statistics: Lester Mitcham, e-mail message to author, February 18, 2011.

Befriended by a rich American couple . . . : O'Donnell 91. See also the Frank Browne website: www.titanicphotographs.com.

Chapter Two

"*Titanic*, April 11th . . .": Hyslop, Donald, Alastair Forsyth, and Sheila Jemima, Titanic *Voices: Memories from the Fateful Voyage* (New York: St. Martin's, 1994) 113.

"The *Titanic* was wonderful . . .": ibid. 132.

Lunch menu: Archbold, Rick, *Last Dinner on the* Titanic (Madison Press: Toronto, 1997) 26.

Photos, diagrams, and descriptions of the gymnasium appear in Beveridge et al., 2:204–206.

"placing one passenger . . .": Winocour 8.

"I enjoyed myself . . . ": Gracie, Archibald, Titanic: *A Survivor's Story* (Chicago: Academy Chicago Publishers, 1998) 5.

Amusements: Beveridge et al. 2: 27–33.

First class cabins: Green, Rod, *Building the* Titanic: *An Epic Tale of Modern Engineering and Human Endeavor* (London: Carlton, 2005) 68–69.

Parlor suites: Beveridge et al. 2: 264–266.

"fourteen trunks . . .": Green 74.

"$30,000 in jewelry": *New York Times*, "Mrs. J. W. Cardeza, *Titanic* Survivor," obituary, August 2, 1939.

"In between . . .": ibid.

Boat Deck: Beveridge et al. 2: 185. Also, David G. Brown, e-mail message to author, February 12, 2011.

Boat Deck: Green 78–79.

"sixty-four lifeboats . . .": Eaton and Haas 32.

A Deck: Beveridge et al. 2:225–258.

Grand staircase and clock: ibid. 233–236.

Grand staircase: ibid. 233–237.

B Deck: ibid. 259–304.

C and D Decks: ibid. 305–386.

E, F, and G Decks: ibid. 387–446.

Tank Top. This is explained more fully in Beveridge et al. 1: 64: "*Titanic* was constructed with a 'double bottom' in which the lowest part of the hull was formed not by a single layer of steel plating, but by a heavily reinforced structure with the vertical keel as its backbone. With the outer bottom plating forming the 'skin' of the ship, the inner bottom plating formed the 'Tank Top,' so named because the resultant structure, together with its longitudinal girders and transverse members, formed a series of tanks."

First class dining: Beveridge et al. 2:157–178.

First class dining menu: Green 67.

Frankie hung on . . . : Goldsmith 10.

"one myth that persists . . .": Beveridge et al. 2: 24.

"We young boys . . .": Goldsmith 10.

"a little higher": British Wreck Commissioner's Inquiry, Day 3, 1837.

"*Titanic*'s 159 furnaces . . .": "Technical Facts about the *Titanic*," Titanic *and Other White Star Line Ships.*

The fourth funnel: Green 48.

Chapter Three

"*On board RMS* Titanic . . .": Behe, George, *On Board RMS* Titanic: *Memories of the Maiden Voyage* (Raleigh: Lulu.com, 2010) 123.

"being seventeen . . .": Thayer, John B., *The Sinking of the S.S.* Titanic (Chicago: Academy Chicago, 1998) 333.

"It was planned. . . .": ibid. 329.

"I remember . . .": Winocour 334.

"I was sitting . . .": Letter from Jack Thayer to Judge and Mrs. Charles L. Long of Springfield, MA, April 23, 1912. Posted on *Encyclopedia Titanica*, October 17, 2000. www.encyclopedia-titanica.org/discus/messages/5811/1155.html.

"It had become . . .": Winocour 334.

"I was up early . . .": Gracie 5.

Photos and descriptions of the swimming bath: Beveridge et al. 2: 413–416.

"Look, Mrs. Goldsmith! . . .": Goldsmith 10.

Singing hymns: Winocour 24.

"the first time . . .": *Encyclopedia Titanica*, Reverend Ernest Courtenay Carter. Second class passenger Reverend Carter and his wife both died in the sinking. See www.encyclopedia-titanica.org/titanic-biography/ernest-courtenay-carter.html.

"It was a brilliant crowd. . . .": Tibballs, Geoff, ed., *The Mammoth Book of the* Titanic: *Contemporary Accounts from Survivors and the World Press* (New York: Carroll & Graf, 2002) 58–59. May Futrelle's account originally appeared in the *Boston Sunday Post,* April 21, 1912.

First class dining saloon: Beveridge et al. 2:366.

"I remember . . .": Tibballs 58–59.

"There was death chill . . .": ibid. 59–60.

"It was all so quiet . . .": Jessop 124.

Guglielmo Marconi's . . . : Booth, John, and Sean Coughlan, Titanic — *Signals of Disaster* (Westbury, UK: White Star, 1993) 25.

Both of *Titanic*'s wireless . . . : ibid. 24.

In the Marconi wireless room: ibid. 25.

Shore stations: ibid.

Wireless messages: Eaton and Haas 113–114.

"The *Titanic* herself . . .": Booth and Coughlan 25–26.

Titanic's call letters MGY . . . : Eaton and Haas 32.

"Captain, *Titanic* . . .": ibid. 114.

"In my fifteen years' experience . . .": Winocour 280.

"I said something . . .": British Inquiry, Day 11, 13615.

"In the event of meeting ice . . .": ibid. 13569.

"really the worst form of ice . . .": ibid. 13560.

"when anyone asks . . .": "Disaster at Last Befalls Capt. Smith," *New York Times*, April 16, 1912.

"If it becomes at all doubtful . . .": British Inquiry, Day 11, 13635.

Chapter Four

"In latitude . . .": Booth and Coughlan 15.

"The wireless operator . . .": Winocour 280–281.

"Above all . . .": Lord, Walter, *The Night Lives On* (New York: Morrow, 1986) 63.

"All right . . .": United States Senate Inquiry, Day 4, FRF046.

"a sort of slight haze.": British Inquiry, Day 15, 17250.

"I reported . . .": United States Senate Inquiry, Day 4, FRF067.

Each second . . . : Quinn, Paul, *Dusk to Dawn: Survivor Accounts of the Last Night on the* Titanic (Hollis, NH: Fantail, 1999) 64.

38 feet a second: Lord, *The Night Lives On* 69.

"I heard the first Officer . . .": British Inquiry, Day 13, 15346.

"Murdoch's hard-a-port order . . .": David G. Brown, e-mail message to author, February 12, 2011. There are several recent books that analyze both the likely sequence of events on the ship's bridge and the traditional version of the crash including Brown's *The Last Log of the* Titanic (Camden, ME: International Marine/McGraw Hill, 2001).

Chapter Five

"It was not a loud crash . . .": Behe 314.

"long grinding sound": Senate Inquiry, Day 7. ALO013.

"great, big mass": British Inquiry, Day 15, 17314.

A dark mass coming through the haze . . . : ibid. Day 4, 2441–2442.

"Shut the dampers!": ibid., Day 3, 665. According to Brown, *The Last Log*, "Closing the dampers on the furnaces was an ordinary precaution for reducing the fires to prevent generating excess steam pressure while the engineers stopped the engines" 76.

George Beauchamp: ibid. 662–677. Also, David G. Brown e-mail message to author, February 12, 2011.

"half ahead": Brown, David G. "Chronology — Sinking of S.S. *Titanic*," downloaded document 22. See also Senate Inquiry, Day 7.

"no damage whatever . . .": British Inquiry, Day 13, 15367.

"I didn't even feel . . .": Winocour 314.

Bride remembered it . . . : ibid.

"absolutely out of breath": Joseph Boxhall's account of his actions after the sinking can be heard in a BBC interview recorded on October 22, 1962, at www.bbc.co.uk/archive/titanic/5049.shtml.

The ship was making water fast: British Inquiry, Day 13, 15370.

"Nothing more than that . . .": Winocour 27–28.

he threw a dressing gown . . . : ibid. 28.

"'I don't suppose it is anything much . . .'": ibid.

"'I expect the iceberg . . .'": ibid. 29.

"'Just run along . . .'": ibid. 30.

"moving very slowly . . .": ibid.

"a curious sense . . .": ibid.

"I cut in . . .": ibid. 315.

"The sensation to me . . .": Hyslop et al. 133.

"'What do you think . . .'": ibid.

"'We had better go . . .'": ibid.

"I heard some terrible noise . . .": Senate Inquiry, Day 13.

". . . just as I was going . . .": ibid.

"I was enjoying . . .": Gracie 14.

". . . there was no commotion . . .": ibid.

"It was a beautiful night . . .": ibid. 15.

"He opened his hand . . .": ibid. 17.

"Two hundred bags of mail": ibid.

"The sudden quiet . . .": Thayer 334.

"going up on deck . . .": ibid. 336.

"There were quite a few people . . .": ibid. 337.

"and then I saw . . .": British Inquiry, Day 4, 3367.

"The downward tipping . . .": David G. Brown, e-mail message to author, February 12, 2011.

"Ironically . . .": Brown, *The Last Log*, 120.

"'Is it really serious?'": British Inquiry, Day 13, 15610.

Chapter Six

"Captain Smith . . . appeared nervous . . .": Behe 356.

Joseph Boxhall's movements . . .": Senate Inquiry, Day 3, JGB432–JGB457.

"We are putting . . .": Eaton and Haas 166.

Most of the room was in steerage . . . : Carpathia: *Encyclopedia Titanica*: www.encyclopedia-titanica.org/ship/154.

"the Electric Spark . . .": Lord, *The Night Lives On* 155.

"It was only a streak of luck . . .": Cottam, Harold, "*Titanic*'s 'C.Q.D.' Caught by a Lucky Fluke," *New York Times*, April 28, 1912.

"Come at once . . .": Booth and Coughlan 2.

"Shall I go to the Captain . . . ?": Cottam, *New York Times*, April 28, 1912.

"Yes. Yes.": ibid.

Cottam informs Rostron: British Inquiry 25388.

"I immediately sent down . . .": ibid. 25391.

Chapter Seven

"There are plenty of boats . . .": Jessop 127.

"plenty of boats . . .": ibid.

"not to make a fuss . . .": Senate Inquiry, Day 16.

"a circle of ships around waiting": ibid.

"We all went . . .": Senate Inquiry, Day 13.

". . . it did not seem . . .": ibid.

"All passengers on deck . . .": Winocour 31.

"We stood there . . .": ibid. 33.

"had come quietly to rest . . .": ibid. 34.

"Suddenly . . . a rocket leapt . . .": ibid. 35.

"Anybody knows . . .": ibid.

"Everyone knew . . .": ibid.

"Say, old man . . .": Lynch 83.

"Shut up! . . .": ibid.

Chapter Eight

"Women and children first . . .": Behe 373–374.

Fourth Officer Boxhall's actions: Some researchers put the time of the first rocket at about 12:31 A.M., others at 12:45 A.M. There is also debate about the exact launch times.

For a discussion on third class passengers' ability to get to the Boat Deck, see the discussion on Passenger Research/ General 3rd Class: Encyclopedia Titanica postings, February 6 to March 21, 2000. www.encyclopedia-titanica.org/discus/ messages/5811/246.html?953663520.

Manpower needed to lower lifeboats: David G. Brown, e-mail message to author, February 12, 2011.

Boiler Room 4: Lord, Night Lives On, 76.

Sent up by Mr. Harvey: British Inquiry, Day 3, 2061.

"sloping down by the head . . .": ibid. 2046–2049.

"fifteen or twenty feet": Senate Inquiry, Day 7.

"It seemed . . .": Thayer 339.

"It was now about 12:45 A.M. . . .": ibid. 338–339.

"People like ourselves . . .": Winocour 339.

"Long and I . . .": ibid. 340.

"Our lifeboat . . .": Gracie 253–254.

"The first touch . . .": ibid.

"The first wish . . .": ibid.

"Someone was shouting . . .": Hyslop et al. 135.

"The third boat . . .": ibid.

"Any ladies . . .": Winocour 37.

"I sat on the edge . . .": ibid.

"Lower aft! . . .": ibid. 38.

A sigh of relief . . . : ibid. 40.

"One of his feet . . .": Gracie 30.

"Leaning out over the rail . . .": ibid. 30–31.

Emily Ryerson affidavit: Senate Inquiry, Day 16.

Boat Deck: Brown, David G. "Chronology — Sinking of the *S.S. Titanic*." E.T. Research 13 June 2009. www.encyclopedia-titanica.org/chronology-sinking-of-ss-titanic.html.

"'Are there any more . . .'": Gracie 34.

"All passengers . . .": ibid. 34–35.

"the final crisis . . .": ibid. 35.

"We stayed a little while . . .": Senate Inquiry, Day 13.

"We went up . . .": ibid.

"I did not say anything . . .": ibid.

"Just a little ways . . .": ibid.

Third class passengers: Quinn, Paul, *Titanic at Two A.M.: Final Events Surrounding the Doomed Line, an Illustrated Narrative with Survivor Accounts* (Hollis, NH: Fantail, 1997) 13.

"There was one . . .": Senate Inquiry, Day 13.

"He said if he could get hold of him . . .": ibid.

Passengers not called to boats: Brown, *The Last Log*, 174.

"to keep them quiet": British Inquiry Project, Day 9, 10185, Testimony of John Hart.

"It was a long trip . . .": Lord, Walter, *A Night to Remember* (New York: Holt, 1955) 55.

"I took them to the only boat . . .": British Wreck Commissioner's Report, Day 9, 9972–10026. Researchers now question Hart's account.

Gates to first class opened: Lord, *A Night to Remember* 74.

Chapter Nine

"Surely . . .": Jessop 132.

By 2 A.M. . . . : Quinn, *Two A.M.* 21.

B Deck flooding: Lester Mitcham, *Encyclopedia Titanica*, Message Board, posted January 15, 2002 www.encyclopedia-titanica.org/discus/messages/5919/8510.html?1011228779.

the beginning of the end: Quinn, *Two A.M.* 29.

"We young kids . . .": Goldsmith 11.

"'If we are going . . .'": ibid. 14.

"Dad put his arm . . .": ibid. 17.

"'No! I'm staying here . . .'": ibid.

"Mother and I . . .": ibid. 19.

"I got hold of them . . .": Senate Inquiry, Day 10.

"Seconds later . . .": Goldsmith 20.

Jack Thayer and Milton Long's location . . .": Winocour 340–341.

"Long and I debated . . .": ibid. 341–342.

"So many thoughts . . .": ibid. 343.

"I only wish . . .": ibid.

"... to know ...": ibid. 69.

"The sight I saw ...": Barratt 123.

Collapsible D: Quinn, *Two* A.M. 28.

"'For God's sake ...'": "Futrelle Met Death Like Hero Wife Says," *Worcester Telegram*, April 20, 1912.

"A few cowards ...": ibid.

"'Hurry up ...'": ibid.

"As we were ready ...": Winocour 296.

"Looking out ...": Behe 180.

"'Right you are!'": ibid.

"The water was pouring in ...": ibid.

"He was a brave man ...": ibid 316.

"Then I remembered ...": ibid.

"'Men you have done ...'": ibid.

"'All ready, sir.'": ibid. 297.

"'Oh, plenty of time yet, sir ...'": ibid.

"The captain was there ...": Senate Inquiry, Day 7.

twenty to thirty feet: Quinn, *Two* A.M. 55.

Roll to port: Brown, "Chronology" 34.

"The *Titanic* had a pressure fuse ...": Quinn, *Two* A.M. 58.

"Just then the ship ...": Winocour 297. Quinn, *Two* A.M. speculates that it was the bulkhead to Boiler Room 4 that gave way, causing the ship to lose buoyancy and causing a chain reaction. 78.

"I just walked ...": British Inquiry, Day 12, 14052.

"What was one boat ...": Gracie 44.

"... the wave ...": ibid. 49.

"before I could get to my feet ...": ibid. 67.

"I went up to them ...": Winocour 317.

It was now about 2:15 A.M. ...: Thayer 343–344.

"It was like standing ...": ibid. 344.

"We had no time ...": ibid. 345.

"... we could see ...": Senate Inquiry, Day 13.

"it was only about five feet ...": ibid.

To see the stages of sinking through the use of a model of the ship, visit Park Stephenson's article and diagrams, "More Questions than Answers, Part 2," at Titanic *Commutator* 30:173 (2006).

Chapter Ten

"The water was intensely cold ...": British Inquiry, Day 12, 14054.

"The cold was terrific ...": Thayer 345.

"It looked ...": ibid. 347.

Breakup of the ship: Lynch, *Illustrated History* 203.

"Striking the water ...": Winocour 298.

"... as fast as I ...": ibid.

"... another couple of minutes ...": ibid.

"The piece of rope . . .": ibid. 299.

"There were men . . .": Winocour 317.

"There was just room . . .": ibid. 318.

"When I got on . . .": Senate Inquiry, Day 13.

Rhoda Abbott: Bracken, Robert, "The Mystery of Rhoda Abbott Revealed," ET Research, 7 June 2004. Web. 7 June 2004 at www.encyclopedia-titanica.org/rhoda-abbott.html.

"Just at the moment . . .": Gracie 46–47.

Chapter Eleven

"I almost thought . . .": Tibballs 94.

"We could see . . .": Goldsmith 20–21.

"It was partly a roar . . .": Winocour 47.

"When the noise was over . . .": ibid. 47–48.

". . . the huge bulk . . .": ibid. 300.

"The huge ship . . ." ibid.

"I now felt . . .": Gracie 75.

"one long continuous . . .": Thayer 348–349.

"The most heartrending . . .": ibid. 349.

"We were utterly surprised . . .": Winocour 48–49.

Robert Hichens: Senate Inquiry, Day 5.

". . . we all thought . . .": ibid. Day 4.

"Mr. Lowe . . .": British Inquiry, Day 2, 439.

3 A.M.: Lord, *A Night to Remember* 102.

"'Give us a hand in . . .'": Senate Inquiry, Day 7.

"He said, 'Is that you, Sam? . . .'": ibid.

"Do you mean to tell me . . .": ibid.

"It made my feet and hands . . .": ibid.

Testimony of Harold G. Lowe: Senate Inquiry Day 5.

Chapter Twelve

". . . the boat we were in . . .": Gracie 192.

"Shouting began from one end . . .": Winocour 40–41.

"Our plan of action . . .": ibid. 41.

"'The sea will be covered . . .'": ibid.

"Our men knew nothing . . .": Gracie 254–255.

"The life preservers . . .": ibid. 257.

"I have no idea . . .": Hyslop et al. 137

"The salt spray . . .": ibid. 137–138.

"We were standing . . .": Thayer 351.

"lowering us . . .": ibid. 352.

"We prayed . . .": ibid.

"In this little boat . . .": Senate Inquiry, Day 13.

"'Lean to the right . . .'": Winocour 301.

"I didn't care what happened . . .": ibid. 319.

"If ever human endurance . . .": ibid. 301.

"just paddling and treading water . . .": British Inquiry, Day 6, 6081.

"Just as it was breaking daylight . . .": ibid. 6085.

"A cook that was on . . .": ibid. 6099.

"Some quietly lost consciousness . . .": Winocour 301.

". . . glory be to God . . .": Gracie 106.

Chapter Thirteen

"Even through my numbness . . .": Winocour 354.

"Knowing that the *Titanic* . . .": Senate Inquiry, Day 1, AHR027.

"I went full speed . . .": ibid. AHR094.

Captain Arthur Rostron's preparations: ibid.

"Engine room full up to the boilers": Eaton and Haas 178.

"Between 2:45 and 4 o'clock . . .": Senate Inquiry, Day 1.

The *Carpathia*'s speed and course: Dave Gittens, "The *Carpathia* Legend," 22 May 2009, *All at Sea with Dave Gittens.*

"The *Carpathia*, waiting for . . .": Thayer 353.

"For us . . .": ibid.

". . . on our starboard side . . .": Gracie 106–107.

"'Come over and take us off . . .'": ibid. 107.

"'Aye, Aye, sir'": ibid.

"It took them ages . . .": Thayer 354.

"Lightoller remained . . .": Gracie 107–108.

"Sea and wind were rising . . .": Winocour 302.

"All night long I had heard . . .": Gracie 258–260.

"It seemed to me . . .": ibid. 111.

"Now to get her safely alongside!": Winocour 302.

"All along the side . . .": Gracie 111.

"All my wet clothing . . .": ibid. 112.

"I was all the time . . .": ibid. 76.

"I was sore to the touch . . .": ibid. 77.

"It was now about . . .": Winocour 354–355.

"It was the first drink . . .": ibid. 355.

"one big heartache . . .": ibid.

"The passengers and crew . . .": ibid. 355–356.

"We could only rush . . .": Hyslop et al. 138.

"By the time . . .": Kuntz 28.

"a short prayer of thankfulness . . .": Senate Inquiry, Day 1.

"After that . . .": Winocour 319.

"Whenever I started . . .": ibid.

"On the afternoon of Tuesday. . .": ibid. 80.

". . . she asked the men . . .": Goldsmith 25.

"all over the ship . . .": ibid. 26.

"Then it all came back to me . . .": ibid.

"I have never seen . . .": Thayer 356.

"What kindness was there . . .": Winocour 303.

"For our dear Tommy Andrews . . .": Jessop 139.

"But there was little . . .": ibid. 140.

"Sir . . .": Winocour 81.

"First . . .": ibid. 81–82.

Chapter Fourteen

"The final docking . . .": ibid. 356.

Word of the disaster: Eaton and Haas 181.

Souvenirs: ibid. 194–197.

"My life-belt . . .": Gracie 108–109.

"I think we all realized . . .": Winocour 83–84.

"I am glad to say . . .": Barratt 113.

"In the dusk of evening . . .": Jessop 140–141.

"Brooklyn, New York . . .": Hyslop et al. 284.

"I read by the papers . . .": Bracken, Robert, "The Mystery of Rhoda Abbott," ET Research, June 7, 2004.

"investigate the causes . . .": Kuntz xvii.

British Wreck Commissioner's Inquiry: Final Report.

"As the sole survivor . . .": Gracie 1.

"The events of the night . . .": "Col. Gracie Dies, Haunted by *Titanic*," *New York Times*, December 5, 1912.

"To my mind . . .": Thayer 330.

Epilogue

"Finding *Titanic* . . .": LaRoe, Lisa Moore, Titanic: *Collector's Edition* (Washington, DC: National Geographic Society, 1999.) 15.

"images of twisted railing . . .": ibid. 13.

"Then it hit us . . .": ibid.

"the stern section . . .": ibid.

"Before leaving the wreck . . .": ibid. 15.

Survivor Letters from the *Carpathia*

"On the waves . . .": Behe 136–137.

"On board the *Carpathia* . . .": Behe 164.

"Dear Mother . . .": Behe 151.

"Our ship struck an iceberg . . .": Behe 146.

"Wednesday, *Carpathia* . . .": Behe 151–152.

Titanic Facts and Figures

Bodies recovered: Courtesy of Bill Wormstedt. To learn more about the recovery of victims, go to "An Analysis of the Bodies Recovered from the *Titanic*," *Bill Wormstedt's* Titanic, 22 October 2000.

❖ PHOTO CREDITS ❖

Cover: *Titanic* painting by Ken Marschall.

Page i: Postcard oilette of the *Titanic*, The Art Archive/Ocean Memorabilia Collection.

Page ii: Iceberg, Library of Congress.

Page iii: Funnels on a White Star Line ship, North Wind Picture Archives.

Pages iv–v: Copy of the last message sent from the *Titanic*, which tells of passengers being put into lifeboats after the ship hit an iceberg, Popperfoto/Getty Images.

Page vi: Iceberg; Library of Congress.

Page vii: *Titanic* in port, Topham/The Image Works.

Pages: viii–ix: Side view of the *Titanic*, ibid.

Foreword

Pages x–xi: Wreck of the *Titanic*, Walt Disney/courtesy Everett Collection.

Pages xii–xiii: Diagram of ship, © The Mariners' Museum/Corbis

Chapter One

Pages xiv–1: Boarding the *Titanic*, Universal Images Group/Getty Images.

Pages 4–5: J. Bruce Ismay and William James Pirrie, National Museums Northern Ireland.

Page 7: *Titanic* in dry dock, Library of Congress.

Pages 8–9: Propellers, ibid.

Page 11: Captain Edward John Smith, Mary Evans Picture Library/Onslow Auctions/The Image Works.

Page 13: Early photograph of *Titanic*'s Café Parisien, Ulster Folk & Transport Museum.

Page 14: Thomas Andrews, National Museums Northern Ireland.

Page 19: *Titanic* leaving Southampton, England, Mary Evans Picture Library/Onslow Auctions/The Image Works.

Page 20: Frank Browne's passage ticket, Universal Images Group/Getty Images.

Chapter Two

Pages 22–23: Promenade Deck, Universal Images Group/Getty Images.

Page 25: Stationary bicycles in the gymnasium, Mary Evans Picture Library/The Image Works.

Pages 28–29: *Titanic*'s gymnasium, akg-images/Universal Images Group/The Image Works.

Page 30: Interior: bed of a luxury cabin, akg-images/Newscom.

Page 31: Father Browne's stateroom, Universal Images Group/Contributor/Getty Images.

Page 33: Second class deck, John Reavenall/Newscom.

Page 35: Grand staircase, Universal Images Group/Getty Images.

Page 38: Illustration of the first class dining room, SSPL via Getty Images.

Page 39: First class dinner menu, The Granger Collection.

Page 42: Funnels on a White Star Line ship, North Wind Picture Archives.

Pages 44–45: Promenade Deck, Universal Images Group/Getty Images.

Chapter Three

Page 46: Reading room, Mary Evans Picture Library/The Image Works.

Pages 50–51: Swimming pool, Universal Images Group/Getty Images.

Pages 54–55: First class dining room, ibid.

Page 58: Harold Bride, Getty Images.

Chapter Four

Page 64: Iceberg in the distance, Library of Congress.

Pages 66–67: Radio telegram, Matthew Cavanaugh/AP Photo.

Chapter Five

Page 72: Chronometer from the bridge of the *Titanic*, Alastair Grant/AP Photo.

Page 75: Wireless operator, Pictorial Press Ltd./Alamy.

Chapter Six

Page 80: Iceberg, 1912, TopFoto/The Image Works.

Pages 86–87: The *Olympic* Wheelhouse, Universal Images Group/ Getty Images.

Page 90: Distress telegram, Public Record Office/HIP/The Image Works.

Chapter Seven

Page 95: Life preserver, Chris Ratcliffe/Bloomberg via Getty Images.

Chapter Eight

Page 103: Diagram of nearby ships, National Archives, Washington, D.C.

Page 104: Women and children boarding a lifeboat, Mary Evans Picture Library/The Image Works.

Page 108: Photo of the lifeboats taken by Father Browne, Bettmann/Corbis.

Chapter Nine

Page 123: Lifeboats, the Illustrated London News Picture Library/ The Bridgeman Art Library.

Page 139: Map of voyage by Heather Saunders.

Chapter Ten

Pages 140–141: Illustration of the *Titanic*, Getty Images.

Chapter Eleven

Pages 148–149: *Titanic* sinking, Popperfoto/Getty Images.

Chapter Twelve

Page 159: Lifeboat Collapsible B, Phillyseaport.org.

Chapter Thirteen

Page 167: Survivors en route to the *Carpathia*, Getty Images.

Page 169: Captain Arthur H. Rostron, Library of Congress.

Page 176: Rope ladder between the *Carpathia* and lifeboat, Roger-Viollet/The Image Works.

Page 179: *Titanic* survivors, Library of Congress.

Pages 180–181: More survivors, Getty Images.

Page 184: Survivor's Marconi telegraph message, PA/Topham/ The Image Works.

Page 185: *Titanic* survivors, Library of Congress.

Page 186: List of the dead, Public Record Office/HIP/The Image Works.

Pages 190–191: *Titanic* lifeboats on deck of the *Carpathia*, North Wind Picture Archives.

Page 192: Crewmembers in life jackets, The Print Collector/ Heritage–Images/The Image Works.

Chapter Fourteen

Pages 194–195: Crowd outside the White Star Line offices in London, England, Mary Evans Picture Library/The Image Works.

Pages 198–199: *New York Times* headline, Getty Images.

Pages 200–201: *New York American* bulletin board, Stapleton Historical Collection/HIP/The Image Works.

Pages 202–203: Crowd outside the White Star Line offices in New York City, akg-images/The Image Works.

Page 204: Newspaper boy, Print Collector/HIP/The Image Works.

Page 206: Harold Bride with injured feet, Mary Evans Picture Library/The Image Works.

Pages 210–211: U.S. Senate Investigating Committee, Library of Congress.

Pages 214–215: Surviving crew members, Getty Images.

Epilogue

Page 218: Dr. Robert Ballard, AP Photo/Mike Kullen.

Pages 220–221: Bow of the wrecked *Titanic*, AP Photo.

☀ INDEX ☀

275

Ismay, Thomas Henry, 3, 230

W

⇝ ACKNOWLEDGMENTS ⇜

A book is like a journey, and I owe thanks to many people who kept me afloat during the writing of Titanic: *Voices from the Disaster*.

I am immensely grateful to the incomparable Lisa Sandell, for her skilled and insightful editing, as well as her unfailing and gracious encouragement. Phil Falco's design brings the words and photos to life in ways I could never have imagined. Thanks to everyone at Scholastic, especially Jody Corbett, Elizabeth Starr Baer, Bonnie Cutler, Emma Brockway in publicity, Rachel Coun, Lizette Serrano, Emily Heddleson, Candace Greene, John Mason, Debbie Kurosz, Elizabeth Parisi, David Levithan, Robin Hoffman, Jennifer Ung, and so many others for their hard work and dedication to bringing books to readers.

Fellow writer and dear friend Debbie Wiles was there at every step of the way, with text messages, phone calls, and e-mails to keep me going, day and night. She no doubt is now a *Titanic* expert herself, having experienced vicariously everything from launching the lifeboats to the harrowing rescue. I am also grateful to Steven Malk, my agent, for his ongoing support and wise counsel, and to Michele Kopfs for helping to create a website, www.deborahhopkinson.com, that conveys my own passionate interest in history.

Although I plunged into *Titanic* research fully, I'm a neophyte in comparison to those who've made a lifelong study of the topic. I owe a debt of gratitude to researchers and enthusiasts worldwide whose dedication, curiosity, and generosity have made learning and writing about this topic so rewarding.

I would like to extend my heartfelt thanks to David G. Brown, author of *The Last Log of the* Titanic, who not only read the manuscript, but generously answered scores of questions and provided nautical explanations. A mariner himself, David's detailed timeline of events was absolutely invaluable and is a must-read for anyone interested in the disaster. I'd sail with Captain Brown any day!

Special thanks also to Bill Wormstedt, author of many articles on the *Titanic*, for reading the manuscript and to Bill, as well as Tad Fitch and George Behe, for allowing us to include their chart "*Titanic* Lifeboats, Launch Times Re-Examined." For this book, Lester Mitcham graciously created a special version of a table that appeared in his fascinating paper "The Statistics of the Disaster." All of this original research is an inspiration to young historians.

It was a delight to correspond with such generous and patient experts. It's not surprising that researchers like these gentlemen spend a lot of time helping others learn about the *Titanic*. And it would be hard to underestimate the time, energy, and commitment that has gone into making the *Encyclopedia Titanica* website and message board, founded by Philip Hind in 1996, such an amazing resource. An example of historical thinking in action, the community is also a model for civil discourse on the Internet. I'm grateful for all the help I have received.

I am extraordinarily lucky to have wonderful friends and family who listened to my stories of lifeboats and ice warnings, including Janice Fairbrother and Bonnie Johnson, Michele Hill,

287

Vicki Hemphill, Ellie Thomas, Nick Toth, Maya Abels, Sara Wright, Sheridan Mosher, Deborah Correa, Eric Sawyer, Kristin Hill, Bill Carrick, and many more. I'm grateful to my wonderful colleagues and friends at Pacific Northwest College of Art, especially the Advancement team: Deniz Conger, Lisa Degrace, Heather Hale, Aidan Krainock, Mariely Lemagne, Melinda Stoops, and Alisha Sullivan. I can't think of anyone I'd rather do the hard work of philanthropy with, day after day. Thanks also to PNCA's leadership: Tom Manley, Nancy Barrows, Greg Ware, and Melissa McClure. I'm grateful to Jacob Krieger for reading a draft of the manuscript and making comments. Writers don't get much social life. But I'd like to thank Cyndi for tea and conversation, and my Clubsport friends, especially Trisha, Roxanne, Gail, Jo, Kathy, and Loren, among others, for just being there on those early Saturday mornings.

And lastly, to Andy, Rebekah, and Dimitri, I love you. You put up with me taking over the kitchen table, piling research books everywhere, and rambling on about watertight doors and poor Mr. Andrews. And while I sometimes stirred to throw the ball for Kona, move Sophie off my lap, or, while we still had her, give our sweet Pea a treat, I certainly didn't do much cooking. Thank you for everything. If I were balancing all night on the upturned bottom of Collapsible B, I can't think of anyone else I'd want with me.

— Deborah Hopkinson, January 2012

➤ ABOUT THE AUTHOR ⧏

Deborah Hopkinson is the author of many award-winning books, including *Sweet Clara and the Freedom Quilt*, winner of the 1994 International Reading Association Award; *A Band of Angels*, an ALA Notable title that also won the Golden Kite Award and a Jane Addams Award Honor; *Under the Quilt of Night*, winner of the Washington State Book Award; *Bluebird Summer*, a Golden Kite Award Honor Book; *Girl Wonder*, winner of the Great Lakes Book Award and a 2004 Jane Addams Award Honor; *Apples to Oregon*, which won the Golden Kite Award; *Abe Lincoln Crosses a Creek*; *Sky Boys: How They Built the Empire State Building*; *A Boy Called Dickens*; and *Annie and Helen*, among many other picture and chapter books.

Deborah's nonfiction works for older readers include *Up Before Daybreak: Cotton and People in America*, which won a Carter G. Woodson Honor Award, and *Shutting out the Sky: Life in the Tenements of New York, 1880–1924*, which was an NCTE Orbis Pictus Award Honor Book, a Jane Addams Peace Award Honor Book, an IRA Teachers' Choice, and a James Madison Award Honor Book.

Deborah received a bachelor's degree in English at the University of Massachusetts and holds a master's degree in Asian Studies from the University of Hawaii at Manoa. She lives near Portland, Oregon, where she serves as Vice President for Advancement for the Pacific Northwest College of Art.

History Speaks: Unforgettable True Tales from Deborah Hopkinson

Harrowing portraits of struggling young immigrants in turn-of-the-century New York City.

★ "Make[s] history come alive."
—*Kirkus Reviews*, starred review

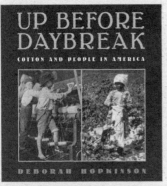

The epic story of the child laborers that built America's cotton empire.

★ "Lively...vivid and personal."
—*Kirkus Reviews*, starred review

The gripping story of the TITANIC and its passengers from the ship's celebrated launch to its cataclysmic icy end.

★ "Riveting."
—*Publishers Weekly*, starred review